THE GOSPEL
AND
ITS WITNESSES

By the same Author

CHRISTIANITY AND MORALITY
THE BOYLE LECTURES FOR 1874 *AND* 1875

FIFTH EDITION, 6s

THE FOUNDATIONS OF FAITH
THE BAMPTON LECTURES FOR 1879

SECOND EDITION, 7s. 6d

PICKERING AND CO., LONDON

THE STUDENT'S EVIDENCES OF CHRISTIANITY

Post 8vo   [*In preparation*

JOHN MURRAY, ALBEMARLE STREET

The Gospel and its Witnesses

SOME OF THE

CHIEF FACTS IN THE LIFE OF OUR LORD

AND THE

AUTHORITY OF THE EVANGELICAL NARRATIVES

CONSIDERED IN LECTURES

CHIEFLY PREACHED AT ST. JAMES'S, WESTMINSTER

By HENRY WACE B.D., D.D.
PREBENDARY OF ST. PAUL'S, PREACHER OF LINCOLN'S INN,
PROFESSOR OF ECCLESIASTICAL HISTORY IN KING'S COLLEGE, LONDON,
CHAPLAIN TO THE ARCHBISHOP OF CANTERBURY.

WIPF & STOCK · Eugene, Oregon

Wipf and Stock Publishers
199 W 8th Ave, Suite 3
Eugene, OR 97401

The Gospel and its Witnesses
Some of the Chief Facts in the Life of Our Lord
and the Authority of the Evangelical Narratives
Considered in Lectures
By Wace, Henry
Softcover ISBN-13: 978-1-7252-9070-9
Hardcover ISBN-13: 978-1-7252-9072-3
eBook ISBN-13: 978-1-7252-9071-6
Publication date 11/2/2020
Previously published by John Murray, 1883

This edition is a scanned facsimile of
the original edition published in 1883.

Inscribed to

THE REV. JOHN EDWARD KEMPE, M.A.

PREBENDARY OF ST. PAUL'S

RECTOR OF ST. JAMES'S, WESTMINSTER

CHAPLAIN IN ORDINARY TO THE QUEEN

BY HIS FORMER CURATE

IN GRATEFUL ACKNOWLEDGMENT

OF HIS GUIDANCE AND SUPPORT

DURING TWENTY YEARS

PREFACE.

THE following Lectures were for the most part preached at St. James's, Piccadilly, in 1881, at the invitation of the Rector, the Rev. Prebendary Kempe; but they have been enlarged and supplemented from Sermons since preached at Lincoln's Inn, and before the University of Oxford. The design of the author was to exhibit the real character and results of modern criticism in respect to the authenticity of the Gospels, and, at the same time, to illustrate the credibility and spiritual significance of the main facts in the Evangelical narratives. Accordingly, after showing in the first two Lectures that the critical enquiries of the last fifty years have failed to establish any objections against the traditional authorship of the four Gospels, he has considered the witness of the Evangelists to the main truths respecting our Lord which are recited in the Creed, and in that summary of the Gospel which St. Peter proclaimed to Cornelius. The Lectures thus treat in succession of our Lord's birth; of the name of

JESUS as signifying the purpose of the Gospel; of our Lord's Ministry of power and mercy; of His atoning Death; of His Resurrection; of His Ascension and future return to judgment; and of the gift of the Holy Spirit. Within the limits determined by the nature of such a series of Lectures, the author has endeavoured to show how the various considerations thus reviewed confirm one another, and combine to support the faith of the Church in the Gospel of our Lord Jesus Christ.

May 1883.

CONTENTS.

LECTURE I.

THE CHRISTIAN CREED AND ITS EVIDENCE.

"The word which God sent unto the children of Israel, preaching peace by Jesus Christ: (He is Lord of all:) that word, I say, ye know, which was published throughout all Judæa, and began from Galilee, after the baptism which John preached; how God anointed Jesus of Nazareth with the Holy Ghost and with power: who went about doing good, and healing all that were oppressed of the devil; for God was with Him. And we are witnesses of all things which He did both in the land of the Jews, and in Jerusalem; whom they slew and hanged on a tree: Him God raised up the third day, and shewed Him openly; not to all the people, but unto witnesses chosen before of God, even to us, who did eat and drink with Him after He rose from the dead. And He commanded us to preach unto the people, and to testify that it is He which was ordained of God to be the Judge of quick and dead. To Him give all the prophets witness, that through His name whosoever believeth in Him shall receive remission of sins." —*Acts* x. 36–43 . . . . *p.* 1

LECTURE II.

THE RESULTS OF MODERN CRITICISM.

"Then returned they unto Jerusalem from the mount called Olivet, which is from Jerusalem a Sabbath day's journey. And when they were come in, they went up into an upper room, where abode both Peter, and James, and John, and Andrew, Philip, and Thomas, Bartholomew, and Matthew, James the son of Alphæus, and Simon Zelotes, and Judas the brother of James. These all continued with one accord in prayer and supplication, with the women, and Mary the mother of Jesus, and with His brethren."—*Acts* i. 12–14 . . . *p.* 23

LECTURE III.

THE BIRTH OF OUR LORD.

"Now the birth of Jesus Christ was on this wise: When as his mother Mary was espoused to Joseph, before they came together, she was found with child of the Holy Ghost."—*Matthew* i. 18 . *p.* 47

LECTURE IV.

THE NAME OF JESUS.

"Thou shalt call His name JESUS, for He shall save His people from their sins."—*Matthew* i. 21 . . . . . . *p.* 68

LECTURE V.

THE MIRACLES OF OUR LORD.

"And when Jesus was entered into Capernaum, there came unto Him a centurion, beseeching Him, and saying, Lord, my servant lieth at home sick of the palsy, grievously tormented. And Jesus saith unto him, I will come and heal him. The centurion answered and said, Lord, I am not worthy that thou shouldest come under my roof: but speak the word only, and my servant shall be healed. For I am a man under authority, having soldiers under me and I say to this man, Go, and he goeth; and to another, Come, and he cometh; and to my servant, Do this, and he doeth it. When Jesus heard it, He marvelled, and said to them that followed, Verily I say unto you, I have not found so great faith, no, not in Israel."—*Matthew* viii. 5-10.
p. 89

LECTURE VI.

THE PASSION AND DEATH OF OUR LORD.

" Whom God hath set forth to be a propitiation through faith in His blood, to declare His righteousness for the remission of sins that are past, through the forbearance of God ; to declare, I say, at this time His righteousness : that He might be just, and the justifier of him which believeth in Jesus."—*Rom.* iii. 25, 26 . . . *p.* 114

LECTURE VII.

THE WITNESS TO OUR LORD'S RESURRECTION.

"This Jesus hath God raised up, whereof we all are witnesses. Therefore being by the right hand of God exalted, and having received of the Father the promise of the Holy Ghost, He hath shed forth this, which ye now see and hear."—*Acts* ii. 32, 33 . . . *p.* 147

LECTURE VIII.

OUR LORD'S RETURN TO JUDGMENT.

" And while they looked stedfastly towards heaven as He went up, behold, two men stood by them in white apparel; which also said, Ye men of Galilee, why stand ye gazing up into heaven ? This same Jesus, which is taken up from you into heaven, shall so come in like manner as ye have seen Him go into heaven."—*Acts* i. 10, 11 . *p.* 172

LECTURE IX.

THE GIFT OF THE SPIRIT.

" Verily, verily, I say unto you, He that believeth on Me, the works that I do shall he do also; and greater works than these shall he do; because I go unto My Father."—*John* xiv. 12 . . *p.* 193

'John sent two of his disciples and said unto Jesus, "Art thou He that should come, or do we look for another?"'

'Jesus answered and said unto them, "Go and shew John again those things which ye do hear and see."'—*St. Matthew* xi. 3, 4.

THE GOSPEL AND ITS WITNESSES

LECTURE I

THE CHRISTIAN CREED AND ITS EVIDENCE

"The word which God sent unto the children of Israel, preaching peace by Jesus Christ: (He is Lord of all:) That word, I say, ye know, which was published throughout all Judæa, and began from Galilee, after the baptism which John preached; How God anointed Jesus of Nazareth with the Holy Ghost and with power: who went about doing good, and healing all that were oppressed of the devil; for God was with Him. And we are witnesses of all things which He did both in the land of the Jews, and in Jerusalem; whom they slew and hanged on a tree: Him God raised up the third day, and shewed Him openly; Not to all the people, but unto witnesses chosen before of God, even to us, who did eat and drink with Him after He rose from the dead. And He commanded us to preach unto the people, and to testify that it is He which was ordained of God to be the Judge of quick and dead. To Him give all the prophets witness, that through His name whosoever believeth in Him shall receive remission of sins."—*Acts* x. 36-43.

THIS passage possesses a special interest, as the original type of Apostolic preaching to the Gentiles —that is, to the world at large, to persons like ourselves, to all in fact who do not approach the Christian revelation from the peculiar point of view occupied by the Jews. It cannot but be regarded as embodying, for our purposes, the sum and substance of the Gospel, and as indicating the central points in the Christian argument. Let us observe, then, that it is a brief and simple summary of the life of our Lord, as recorded in the four Gospels, supplemented by a statement of what He commanded His Apostles to preach after His resurrection. In slight but vivid details, all the essential points of those narratives and of the Saviour's last commands are sketched—His ministry of grace and power, His miracles of mercy and of healing, His crucifixion, His resurrection and His open manifestation to chosen witnesses, His declaration to the Apostles that it is He who was ordained of God to be the Judge of quick and dead, and the assurance that whosoever believed in Him should receive remission of sins. In these few momentous facts lies, according to St. Peter, the whole essence of the Gospel; and that essence is the supernatural character of Jesus Christ, His miraculous powers, His authority to forgive sins, His commission to judge the quick and the dead. In strict harmony with this cardinal example of Apostolic preaching, the Christian Creed, a confession of which has from the earliest ages been the condition of baptism and of admission into the Church, has consisted of a summary of these same facts. One of its earliest forms, that of the primitive Roman Church, ran as follows: 'I believe in God the Father Almighty, and in Jesus Christ His only Son our Lord, who was born of the Holy Ghost and the Virgin Mary, who was crucified under Pontius Pilate and was buried; on the third day he rose again from the dead; He ascended into heaven, and sitteth at the right hand of the Father, from whence He shall come to judge the quick and the dead; and I believe in the Holy Ghost, in the holy Church, the forgiveness of sins, and the resurrection of the flesh.'*

A Christian, accordingly, is a man who believes in these facts, past, present, and future. He is not merely a man who submits himself to the moral teaching of Christ; though that of course is involved in the belief in Him as the Judge of quick and dead—a belief which gives to that teaching an absolutely supreme authority. But, to be a Christian, a man must regard our Lord as having exerted in the past the power and influence which the Gospels record, as exercising a similar influence in the present, and as destined to exercise it with infinite majesty and might in the future. Under this belief, the Christian surrenders himself

---

* See Gebhardt and Harnack, *Apostolic Fathers*, Fasc. I. part 2, p. 115, and an article by Dr. Salmon in the *Contemporary Review* for August 1878.

to Christ for life and death, in sure and certain hope that, through Him, he is reconciled with God, that he will be purged by his Saviour's supernatural grace and power from the moral evil which besets him to the last, and that hereafter he will be raised in purity of soul and incorruption of body to a life of full communion with the truth, the goodness, and the love of the Divine nature. This is the blessed creed which we contemplate in the series of the great festivals of the Christian year, and which reaches its culmination at the two festivals between which we stand—those of Easter and Whitsuntide.

Now, this being the case, it appears that the whole edifice of Christian faith rests upon the foundation of the historic truth of the life and ministry of our Lord, as summarized by St. Peter in this passage, and as narrated in the Gospels; and in these days, when we are daily called upon to give to ourselves, if not to others, a reason of the faith that is in us, it seems of increasing importance we should clearly realize that this is the main question which is practically at issue. Great service has been done, and is still being done, by those who have vindicated the harmony of the great doctrines of Christian theology with the constitution of nature and of man, and who have brought into prominence the immense presumption in favour of our faith afforded by the course of history and by the beneficent influence of Christianity on mankind. Considerations of such a nature are well fitted to be a stay and support to souls in many moments and moods of anxious doubt, during which the answer to other difficulties is for a while obscure; and they must always form an essential part of the Christian argument. A creed which is to command our allegiance must be in harmony with the existing facts of life, must explain them, control them, animate them. But still, when all this is done and said, we must again and again come back to the few facts we have just reviewed—to the simple preaching of St. Peter to Cornelius; to the question whether, as a matter of fact, Jesus of Nazareth was anointed by God with the Holy Ghost and with power; whether He rose from the grave, and ordered His Apostles to proclaim Him as Judge of quick and dead. This, after all, is our one message as Christian ministers. We not only urge upon you certain moral or spiritual truths, but we bring a message to you from the man Christ Jesus, who declared Himself also to be God, and who proved Himself to possess the authority He claimed, not only by His marvellous teaching, but by His visible supremacy over all the powers of nature. We call on you for this reason, as has been said, to surrender yourselves to Him, to obey Him, to trust in Him, to pray to Him— to appeal to Him for daily support, guidance, chastisement, purification—for all the grace which your moral and spiritual and intellectual and bodily nature needs, and to commend yourselves confidently in death to His merciful hands. And if you ask what are our credentials for this gracious, but wonderful and supernatural invitation, we have, and we can have, but one—that the facts recited by St. Peter in the text, and the narratives in the Gospels, are faithful records of the life and deeds and words of the Person of whom we speak.

Accordingly, it is natural and reasonable that, in the course of the present century, the attention of all who take a serious interest in religious truth should have more and more been concentrated on the question of the authenticity of the books of the New Testament, and on the credibility of the account there preserved to us of the life and work of our Lord. The question was first seriously raised, at least in its present import, at the close of the last century; and since then it has passed through various forms, until, in our own time, it has culminated in a series of attempts to give an account of our Lord's life which should be reconcilable with common experience and with the ordinary course of the laws of nature. The Christian must be justly indignant with the spirit by which some of those attempts have been marked, and by the tone of many rationalistic writers on particular points; but it would, I think, be unjust not to admit that it was not only natural, but just and proper, that questions of this nature should be raised and fairly considered, in view of the increased knowledge which has been gained during the last two centuries both of nature and of the facts of human history. The development of natural science has placed miracles in a new light; it can hardly, I think, be denied that it has increased the wonder of them, and it has in proportion enhanced their *primâ facie* improbability. At the same time the advance of criticism in other departments of history and literature has compelled us to reject as legendary stories, as myths or poetical fancies, many narratives respecting obscure parts of history which were formerly accepted without hesitation. It was impossible that serious men should not ask themselves whether it was conceivable that any such legendary process had contributed to produce the marvellous and superhuman stories in the Gospels, and whether the evidence on which we were asked to believe in violations of all ordinary experience would bear the strain. It was a natural consequence of human infirmity that in some cases these questions should be raised with undue audacity, and with an imperfect power of appreciating the moral conditions of the problem. If, as must needs be said, German critics have been often rash, arbitrary, deficient in spiritual and historical penetration—for on so serious a subject it is necessary to speak plainly—their rashness has not less often been a perversion of a very noble quality, perhaps peculiarly characteristic of their nation — of that intrepidity which marked the great hero of the Reformation, and of an impetuous effort to grasp the truth, whatever the apparent cost. The result of their errors, as of many another temporary aberration in the course of the history of theology, has been, on the whole, to bring into clearer light the old truth, and to render more unassailable for the future the cardinal facts of the Christian revelation. But the process has been a perilous one, and has involved for the time a shaking of the foundations of faith, which has, of late years, been severely felt among ourselves. By the brilliant French writer, M. Renan, and by the author of a book called 'Supernatural Religion' among ourselves, the doubts in question have of late years been given vivid expression. At the same time the main points at issue have been so thoroughly argued that it is possible to point to some definite conclusions; and an attempt may not be inopportune to present, in a simple and direct form, the grounds on which we can take our stand in proclaiming, in all its wonder and all its simplicity, the old message of St. Peter respecting the life, the work, and the present power of Christ.

Now, there is one remark to be made at the outset which seems to deserve particular consideration. It is that, among those who have conducted this great controversy, Christian writers alone have approached the subject from an impartial point of view. A different impression no doubt prevails, and it is a common reproach against us that we enter on the discussion with a special interest in favour of the old faith. Of course we do; and it would be a shame to us if we did not. We have the same interest in believing in the truth of the Christian creed that all men have for believing in the truth of any cause with which the civilization they inherit is indissolubly bound up, for which those whom they love and admire best in the world have shed their blood, and with which the deepest and purest and most elevating of their feelings are united. It would be a bitter thing no doubt, and bitter to others than Christians—it would be a shock to human nature, and would shake our faith in the very trustworthiness of our faculties—to have to recognize that the self-sacrifice of Christian martyrs and the devoted lives of Christian saints, inseparably united as they are, in a manner presented by no other religion, with all that is noblest and most progressive in history, with the highest hopes of the human race even for this world—to have to recognize, I say, that all this was founded upon a series of illusions. But nevertheless, none have the right to say of us, any more than they have a right to presume respecting any other men, that we are disqualified by our prejudices from recognizing plain facts. It is facts that we want, and nothing else. Our creed, as has already been said, is a creed of facts; and every light that can be thrown on the evidence for them is welcome to us.

On the other hand, we are justified in saying of the principal writers among our antagonists—for they say it of themselves—that they are so far from entering on the consideration of the subject impartially, that they actually prejudge the very question in dispute. They say, and it is the cardinal and ever-recurring principle of their objections, that miracles and supernatural facts cannot have happened; and that this consideration, taken alone, renders it necessary to treat the narratives of the Gospels as legendary. As illustrations of this attitude of mind, it may be sufficient to mention three leading writers: Strauss, the notorious author of the mythical theory of the Gospels; Baur, the distinguished leader of the Tübingen school; and lastly M. Renan. Strauss, in his final work on this subject, reiterated that the main difficulty in accepting the narratives of the Gospels as historical is that they assume the existence of a personality in our Lord, and recognize the operation of powers in the course of His life, to which we have no parallel in any other history.* Of course we have not—that is the very Christian contention; but to assume that because no such personality and no such deeds are recorded in any other history, therefore they could not have occurred in the case of our Lord, is to beg the whole question at issue—it is to say that no amount of evidence to the narratives of the Gospels would be of any value. Or, as Strauss puts it in another form, 'that which cannot happen did not happen;'† and accordingly the narratives of the Gospels must be explained away by some device or other.

The case is practically the same with Baur. While sympathizing with Strauss, he objected to him that he had not sufficiently investigated the authenticity and date of the Gospels. Strauss laid the stress of the argument on the inherent incredibility of the history; Baur, on the other hand, endeavoured to show that the Gospels were of very late origin, and consequently could not be regarded as valid testimony to the occurrence of the facts. But, after all, the decisive argument, even for him, is that the contents of the Gospels are miraculous and impossible. In his own words, 'The cardinal argument for the

---

* *Das Leben Jesu für das Deutsche Volk bearbeitet*, 3rd ed. 1876, p. 145.

† See also *Das Leben Jesu kritisch bearbeitet*, 4th ed. § 16; *Criterions of what is unhistorical in the Evangelical narrative*.

later origin of our Gospels remains always this—
that each of them for itself, and still more all of
them together, relate so much in the life of Jesus in
a manner in which in reality it is impossible for it
to have happened.'* In other words, Baur, a man
of immense learning and originality, starts on this
momentous enquiry with the prejudgment that the
narratives of the Gospel are impossible; and naturally
he is at no loss to invent theories—most of which,
however, have since been surrendered by his suc-
cessors—as to their composition.

Lastly, as to M. Renan, it is only necessary to quote
one sentence from the preface to the thirteenth edition of his 'Life of Jesus,' in which his work assumed
its final form.† 'At the foundation,' he says, 'of
every discussion of similar matters lies the question of
the supernatural. If miracles and the inspiration of
certain books are a reality, my method is detestable.
If, on the other hand, miracles and the inspiration
of books are beliefs destitute of reality, my method
is a good one. But the question of the supernatural
is decided for us with a complete certainty by this
single reason—that there is no room for believing in
a thing of which the world does not offer any ex-
perimental trace.' Accordingly, he too is obliged to
invent a theory of his own to account for the narra-

---

* *Kritische Untersuchungen über die Kanonischen Evangelien*, 1847; p. 530.

† Page ix.: 15th ed. 1876.

tives of the Gospels, on the supposition of their being legendary. Neither of these well-known writers, in other words, approaches the subject with an open mind. The main question—the question of the trustworthiness of the authors of the Gospels—is settled in advance, not by reference to testimony or criticism, but by an *à priori* supposition: they combine in saying, with Strauss: These things cannot have happened; therefore they did not happen.

The Christian writer, on the other hand, says: 'I am not prepared to say beforehand what may or may not have happened; what is possible and what is impossible. I want simply to know what did happen; and I am prepared to accept good evidence on the subject, however surprising the events to which it bears testimony.' In view of these facts, which are proclaimed in the very face of all the chief negative arguments on this subject, are we not justified in saying that the impartiality is on our side, the prejudice and the assumptions on the other? Of course, if we could be sure that a miracle was inconceivable, the method of rationalistic writers would, as M. Renan says, be justified. But whilst it can be said, in the words of Professor Huxley in his book on Hume, that 'no event is too extraordinary to be possible, and therefore if by the term miracle we mean only extremely wonderful events, there can be no just grounds for denying the possibility of their occurrence,' * no such assumption will be accepted by thoughtful men. We are not accustomed to decide these matters upon abstract theories of possibilities and impossibilities. We want simply to know what is the evidence on the subject; and that has been, and is still, the attitude of all English theologians of distinction.

It is, in short, a fact of the utmost importance for a broad estimate of the value of negative criticism respecting the authenticity of the books of the New Testament, that such criticism has throughout been thus avowedly prompted by a prejudice against the facts in dispute. To quote a legal phrase, the questions put by critics like Strauss, Baur, or Renan have been essentially leading questions; the tone of the reply has been anticipated, and the witness has been unduly pressed to say what was expected. Of this there is a striking illustration in the perpetual tendency of such criticism to push its conclusions too far even for its own purposes, and consequently to be continually driven to recantations. It may be worth while to refer to one conspicuous instance of this tendency to prove too much, which has been afforded of late by a book to which reference has been already made, 'Supernatural Religion.' That

---

* Page 134.

work, like those of the three great critics already named, starts with an argument to show that miracles are impossible, and then, in this spirit, proceeds to examine the evidence for the early existence of the Gospels; and an immense amount of ingenuity is expended in explaining away every evidence that they could have existed in their present form before the latter part of the second century. Now, one important part in this argument relates to the heretic Marcion, who flourished about the year 140. He was said by tradition to have formed a Gospel to suit his own views, by taking our Gospel of St. Luke, and cutting out of it parts which were not in accordance with his principles. If so, St. Luke's Gospel must have existed, and must have been a work of authority, in the first quarter of the second century. The writer of 'Supernatural Religion' accordingly has to explain this tradition away; and he expends more than fifty pages in the effort. But in his 'complete edition,' published in 1879, although he leaves these fifty pages, as he says, 'nearly in their former shape, in order that the true nature of the problem may be better understood,' he is nevertheless obliged to confess that a work recently published by Dr. Sanday has proved that his conclusions on this point were mistaken, that his previous hypothesis was untenable, that St. Luke's Gospel was substantially in the hands of Marcion, and that consequently it must have been composed some time before 140 A.D.* If some credit is due to the candour which makes this admission, it is difficult to know what is to be said of the singular procedure of leaving nearly unaltered a mass of argument all directed to a conclusion now acknowledged to be false; but it will be felt that such a result damages fatally the whole process of which it is an example. A book is written, of which the object, from one end to the other, is to prove that we have no reason to believe that St. Luke's Gospel, any more than any other Gospel, existed before a very late date, and the author discovers after his sixth edition that, with respect to that Gospel at all events, the whole argument is fallacious. He had undertaken to prove too much, and in proportion to the success with which he credits himself is the damage inflicted by a clear proof of failure in a cardinal point.

In this connection it will be interesting to refer to a discovery which has of late attracted much attention among scholars. Even if it be too soon to assume that the results it has hitherto been deemed to involve are conclusively established, it none the less affords a striking example of the rashness of such criticism as we have been considering.

---

* Vol. II. p. 138.

AND ITS EVIDENCE

It relates to a work of the nature of a harmony of the Four Gospels, which tradition had always ascribed to Tatian, the disciple of St. Justin Martyr. Now as Justin flourished in the middle of the second century, and the author of *Supernatural Religion* contended that it was impracticable to find 'a single distinct trace of any of the Synoptic Gospels, with the exception of the third, during the first century and a half after the death of Jesus'*— that is to say, before the year 180 A.D.—it was imperative for him to contend that our Gospels were not used by St. Justin. But if Tatian, one of Justin's disciples, composed a kind of harmony out of our four Gospels, and out of those alone, it would be incredible that they were not known to his master, and were not recognized by him as authoritative. Accordingly this author labours in his usual style to explain away the evidence that Tatian's harmony—or Diatessaron, as it was called —was of the character hitherto generally believed. He urged that 'there is no authority for saying that Tatian's Gospel was a harmony of Four Gospels at all;' and that the natural explanation of the various reports is to be found 'in the conclusion that Tatian did not compose any harmony at all, but simply made use of the same Gospel as his master Justin Martyr, namely, the Gospel according

---

* Vol. II. p. 246. Completed edition, 1879.

to the Hebrews.' In short, we were told, it was
'obvious that there is no evidence of any value connecting Tatian's Gospel with those in our Canon.'*

The pleas thus advanced were met by Bishop
Lightfoot, on the basis of the information then
available, with sufficient conclusiveness;† but by
the recent discovery to which we have alluded, if
we may trust what has hitherto seemed the unanimous consent of scholars, at home and abroad, the
author's contention has been still more completely
overthrown. Through the agency of the Mechitarist
Fathers at Venice a translation was published of
a work preserved in the Armenian language, which
has been generally recognized, by critics belonging to all schools of thought, as the commentary
which a Syrian father of the fourth century—St.
Ephraem—was believed to have written on Tatian's
Diatessaron. By this commentary, it is generally
admitted that we have been placed in possession of the Diatessaron of Tatian, with sufficient fulness, at all events, to judge of its general relations
to our Four Gospels. The result is that Tatian's
work appears to have been a close welding together
of the four Canonical Gospels. For instance, it commences with John i. 1–5, and proceeds to Luke i. 5.
John i. 14, Luke i. 5–77, Matt. i. 18–25, and so

---

* *Supernatural Religion,* Vol. II. pp. 154–7.
† *Contemporary Review,* May, 1877.

on. One of the leading scholars of Germany, Dr. Harnack, who is entirely unprejudiced in favour of traditional views, says that they are so closely interwoven, so ingeniously spun together, that nowhere, so to say, is any seam visible.* The work, indeed, was not a harmony in the sense of the complete text of all four Gospels being harmonized; it seems to have been designed and used as a concise and convenient summary of them; but it did use all of them, and used no other source. The main fact, accordingly, for which orthodox critics have contended on this subject is now generally acknowledged, even by rationalistic critics abroad. Tatian is admitted as a decisive witness to the acceptance of our Four Gospels in the time of Justin Martyr. In other words, our Four Gospels, and only our four, are allowed to have been the recognized authorities respecting the life and ministry of our Lord at a time when their very existence is denied by the author of 'Supernatural Religion.' That book has received so much unwarranted attention in this country that it seemed worth while to notice, in passing, its proved untrustworthiness; and in point of fact the conclusions which its author asserts with such positiveness are as much in conflict with

---

* In an article in Brieger's *Zeitschrift für Kirchengeschichte*, Vol. IV. 1881, p. 476.

a great deal of the most unsparing criticism of the present day as they are with Christian traditions.

This, however, is no unusual example of the fate by which, sooner or later, negative criticism is overtaken. In the last work on the life of our Lord, written by one of the most learned of German scholars, Dr. Bernhard Weiss, occurs a striking testimony to this effect. Dr. Weiss, indeed, is an earnest believer in Christian truth; but while the extent and accuracy of his learning is unquestioned, he proclaims, at the outset of his book, that he does not regard his faith as dependent upon the authenticity of the Gospels, and he does not scruple to treat them as occasionally inaccurate. His testimony, therefore, with respect to the actual results of criticism may be accepted as impartial; and this is what he says respecting the objections raised by criticism against the external testimonies to the fourth Gospel:—
' Baur maintained that before the last quarter of the second century, no traces of the fourth Gospel could be found; but his disciples have been compelled, step by step, to concede one after another of the testimonies against which he contended. Every new discovery since his day—the Philosophumena with their rich Johannine citations out of Gnostic writings, the conclusion of the Clementines with the history of the man born blind, the Syrian Commentary on Tatian's Diatessaron—has definitely confuted

contentions of criticism which had been long and obstinately upheld.'*

The lesson to be drawn from such instances of the failure of one critical theory after another is sufficiently obvious. They are but the most recent examples of the general truth that no alternative theory to the traditions of the Christian Church respecting the authorship of the Gospels has ever held its ground, and that no definite fact in opposition to those traditions has ever been established, even to the general satisfaction of negative critics themselves. In view of this result, such traditions remain in possession of the authority which is due to every witness whose statements have never varied, and in whose evidence no inconsistency or untruth has been established, even by the most prolonged cross-examination, or by further enquiry. The uniform testimony of the earliest Christian antiquity is that St. Matthew, St. Mark, St. Luke, and St. John were the authors of the Gospels which bear their names; and all other explanations of the origin of those Gospels have either destroyed one another, or have been overthrown by new discoveries. This broad fact might alone be sufficient to afford us a practical foundation for our faith. But I propose in the next Lecture to examine more particularly

---

* *Das Leben Jesu*, 1882, Vol. I. p. 92.

the results of critical enquiry respecting each of our Gospels, as illustrated by the statements of the most famous unbeliever of our day—M. Renan. With his assistance, it will be possible, without following in detail all the thorny paths of the criticism of the present century, to estimate the general value of its results. The long debate on this subject has, in fact, at last reached a point at which even simple readers may sufficiently see their way, provided they approach the subject without those prejudices by which, as we have seen, the arguments of negative criticism are marred. In subsequent Lectures, we will consider the leading facts of our Lord's ministry on earth as they are summarized by St. Peter in the text, and recited in the creeds of the Church, with reference at once to their spiritual significance and to their credibility. In pursuing such an enquiry we should be led to a profitable contemplation of our Lord's character, of His deeds and words; and we shall, I trust, be enabled to place a more implicit and unhesitating faith in those grand facts, those marvellous exhibitions of divine power, on which our faith as Christians is based. May God grant us this blessing, through Jesus Christ our Lord!

LECTURE II

THE RESULTS OF MODERN CRITICISM

"Then returned they unto Jerusalem from the mount called Olivet, which is from Jerusalem a sabbath day's journey. And when they were come in, they went up into an upper room, where abode both Peter, and James, and John, and Andrew, Philip, and Thomas, Bartholomew, and Matthew, James the son of Alphæus, and Simon Zelotes, and Judas the brother of James. These all continued with one accord in prayer and supplication, with the women, and Mary the mother of Jesus, and with His brethren."—*Acts* i. 12–14.

It has been shown in the previous Lecture that all the important objections to the authenticity and credibility of the Gospel narratives, as we possess them, all the critical arguments which have been prominent during the present century, have started from the assumption that anything miraculous and supernatural is incredible, and that therefore any documents which profess to contain a record of it must be, in some degree, legendary, and their accounts must need to be explained away. The consequence is that no hostile critic of the Gospel history has approached the subject impartially, and Christian writers alone are willing to estimate without prejudice the testimony offered, and to accept as facts what may thus be established. Some striking instances were also given of the errors into which critics have been betrayed by these prejudices, and of the damage which has been inflicted on their arguments by every successive discovery in early Christian literature. In the present Lecture I propose to enquire more particularly into the practical results of modern criticism respecting the Four Gospels, and to ask how far any conclusions have really been established which are adverse to our belief in the authenticity and credibility of those books.

For this purpose I shall not presume to rely upon any arguments I might myself urge in answer to sceptical critics. It will be sufficient to appeal to the evidence of a witness who is familiar with the whole controversy, who is a master of all the branches of learning connected with it, and who is not only unprejudiced in favour of Christian belief, but is himself the most famous unbeliever of our day. That witness is M. Renan. The interpretation which he places upon the evidence he feels obliged to admit, the manner in which, under the influence of his rationalistic prejudices, he explains away its natural effect, in no way affect the character and the significance of the admissions themselves. We are concerned, at present, simply with the nature of the testimony with which we have to deal. When that is substantially ascertained, we shall be justified in interpreting the evidence ourselves. What we wish to know, in the first instance, is how far modern criticism has seriously succeeded in establishing solid objections against the constant belief of the Church that we possess in the four Gospels the evidence of contemporaries and eye-witnesses. On this point M. Renan is an authority to whom sceptical critics, at all events, cannot fairly demur. If their contentions have not been established, even in the main, to his satisfaction, Christian writers, or apologists—if any one prefers so to call them—can hardly be accused of orthodox prejudices for being of a similar opinion.

Now the third Gospel offers peculiar advantages for entering upon this question. The book of the Acts of the Apostles purports to be by the same writer; and the latter book, from the manner in which the pronoun 'We' is used in its later chapters in describing some of the journeys of St. Paul, affords internal evidence of unique value respecting its authorship. It is well known what has been the uniform tradition of the Church upon the subject, as well as how vehemently it has been attacked by the chief sceptical critics of Germany. If the book of the Acts of the Apostles was written by a friend and companion of St. Paul, the chief theories of Baur and his school at once fall to the ground, and accordingly they have directed ceaseless assaults against its authenticity. How far have they succeeded in establishing their case to the satisfaction of a scholar like M. Renan? They have absolutely failed. After reviewing these criticisms, he says in the introduction to his work on the Apostles :* 'Must we be checked by these objections? I think not; and I persist in believing that the final composition of the Acts of the Apostles is due to the disciple of St. Paul, who says "we" in the last chapters. All the difficulties, however insoluble they may appear, ought, if not to be dismissed, at least to be held in suspense, in presence of an argument so decisive as that which results from that word "we."' He further considers that the tradition is correct, according to which this disciple was St. Luke, and concludes :† 'We think, therefore, that the author of the third Gospel and of the Acts is in all reality Luke, the disciple of Paul.' So again, in the introduction to his 'Life of Jesus,' he says it is evident that if the titles of the four Gospels are correct they at least carry us back to the half-century which followed the death of Jesus; and he proceeds :‡ 'As to Luke doubt is scarcely possible. The Gospel of Luke is a regular composition, founded on previous documents. It is the work of a man who chooses, curtails, combines. The author of this Gospel is certainly the same as

---

* *Les Apôtres* 1866, p. xiv.   † p. xviii.
‡ *Vie de Jésus*, 1876, p. xlix.

the author of the Acts of the Apostles. But the author of the Acts appears to be a companion of St. Paul, a description which agrees completely with Luke.' He adds that he knows that more than one objection can be raised to this statement; but he considers that one thing at least is beyond doubt—though nothing has been more vehemently doubted in Germany—namely, 'that the author of the third Gospel and of the Acts is a man of the second apostolic generation, and this suffices for our purpose'—that is for the purpose of showing that, at the least, the Acts of the Apostles 'carries us back to the half-century which followed the death of Jesus.' But, as we have seen, in his later work on 'The Apostles,' he avows his own opinion unshaken that the author is St. Luke. M. Renan further assumes, from internal evidence, that the Gospel was written after the siege of Jerusalem. His reasons for this opinion might be shown to be very insufficient; but it is enough for our purpose that he says it was written not long afterwards—that is, not long after the year 70—within the lifetime, therefore, of Apostles and contemporaries of our Lord. According to the ordinary computation, our Lord was crucified in the year 30, at the age of thirty-three. Persons, therefore, who were actually contemporary with Him would have been alive at the time St. Luke wrote, and in earlier years he would have been in communication with numbers of such persons. We cannot but fully adopt M. Renan's own words when he adds, 'We are here, then, upon solid ground; for we have before us a work proceeding entirely from the same hand, and marked by the most perfect unity.'

Now the vast import of this admission will be readily apparent. The intimacy between St. Paul and St. Luke was peculiarly close and prolonged. We know from St. Paul's Epistles, that St. Luke possessed his complete confidence; and we cannot therefore but conclude that St. Luke's narrative, both in the Acts of the Apostles and in the Gospel, is supported by the knowledge and the belief of St. Paul. Nor of St. Paul only; for St. Paul, and St. Luke with him, were in intimate association with other Apostles and Evangelists. St. Luke, for instance, according to the evidence afforded by those passages in the Acts of the Apostles to which reference has been made, accompanied St. Paul on his last visit to Jerusalem, and during that visit, at any rate, would have had constant opportunities for communication with the other Apostles who were living there, and probably also with relations of our Lord, including the Virgin Mary, His mother. Unless, therefore, we disbelieve in the veracity of St. Luke—which, it may be safely said, no serious person does—we have in his Gospel a faithful report of direct contemporary and Apostolic testimony respecting the facts which he records. He tells us in his prologue that many records of that testimony already existed; and during his companionship with St. Paul he must have been in a most favourable position for making enquiries respecting such statements, and obtaining supplementary information. He therefore declares in his preface the simple fact, when he says that he had been in a position to obtain a perfect understanding of all things from the very first. This, let me repeat, is not a contention which I am endeavouring to uphold against the general consent of critics; it is not the argument of a Christian controversialist or apologist alone; it is the admission of the most prominent representative of disbelief in the ancient Christian creed in the present day. The result is to justify us in concluding that criticism has established nothing, at all events, against the authenticity of the Gospel of St. Luke, and to assure us that we have in it a record of the narratives and convictions of eye-witnesses.

Now, this consideration leads us a long way back, and throws great light on the authority to be attributed to the other Gospels, and particularly to those of St. Matthew and St. Mark. Not to trouble you with the details of a critical argument, it will be more than enough to accept what M. Renan proceeds to allow: 'In general,' he says, 'the Gospel of St. Luke appears to be of a later date than the two first, and has the character of having been more carefully finished.' But he admits there is no doubt, from the testimony of one of the earliest Christian writers, Papias, that certain documents were written by both St. Matthew and St. Mark which corresponded, in their substantial character, to the two Gospels we now possess under those names.' He considers that the original form of them has been added to and modified, but nevertheless, in his opinion, St. Matthew 'deserves an exceptional confidence' in his report of our Lord's discourses; and as for St. Mark's Gospel, it is 'full of minute observations, proceeding without doubt from an eye-witness;' and there is nothing, he adds, 'to conflict with the report of Papias, that this eye-witness, who had evidently followed Jesus, who had loved Him and watched Him closely, and had preserved a vivid image of Him, was the Apostle St. Peter himself.'*

It will probably be felt to be more satisfactory, for the purposes of our present argument, to adopt these admissions from a witness hostile to the belief of the Church, than to urge on our own part the arguments which might be adduced in favour of still more definite conclusions. There seems a vague

---

* *Vie de Jésus,* pp. l., lxxxi., lxxxiii.

feeling abroad—a feeling based, probably, on reiterated assertion rather than on careful reading—that there is a general consent of unbiassed criticism against the early date of the Gospel narratives, and consequently against our possessing in them the reports of eye-witnesses and of friends of eye-witnesses. It seems, therefore, of the highest importance it should be well understood that, in the deliberate and matured opinion of a person like M. Renan, there is no such critical presumption against the general authority of the Gospels; but that, on the contrary, although he thinks the Gospels of St. Matthew and St. Mark have been in some degree altered from their original form, the records of our Lord's discourses in the one Gospel may be received with peculiar confidence, and the reports of His actions in the Second Gospel bear the mark of proceeding from an eye-witness, who most probably was St. Peter himself. No wonder that he adds, 'In conclusion, I admit the four canonical Gospels as serious documents. They go back to the age which followed the death of Jesus.'* A broad result of this kind is clearly worth a great deal more than any qualifications with which, to meet his own ideas of what is possible or impossible, a critic may accompany it. For all purposes of ordinary historic evidence—and for our present argument it

---

* *Vie de Jésus*, lxxxi.

is unnecessary to push the admission further—it will, we think, be felt that if St. Matthew may be specially trusted respecting our Lord's words, and St. Mark gives the report of an eye-witness respecting his deeds, and St. Luke affords a connected review of both, according to the evidence of Apostles and contemporaries, the record of His ministry which results from the combined evidence of the first three Gospels may be accepted in all its main outlines as supported by the most direct evidence. There is no such material difference between the records of our Lord's deeds in St. Matthew and St. Mark as to make the variations on which M. Renan afterwards dwells of any considerable importance. The story in each Gospel is substantially the same ; and if one of the three Gospels proceeded from an eye-witness, or was the record of an eye-witness's report, there is no reason why the other two should not have proceeded from a similar authority. The great fact which remains, at the close of the long critical debate of the last two generations, is that in the Gospels we do possess accounts of our Lord's life and ministry written either by Apostles themselves, or by companions of Apostles—by persons, that is, who had either themselves witnessed our Lord's deeds and heard His words, or who were in intimate association with those who had.

The admission just quoted from M. Renan

applies, it will be observed, to the Gospel of St. John, as well as to the first three Gospels; but the position of criticism on this latter point is so remarkable as to deserve especial attention. M. Renan's opinion is perhaps the most extraordinary of all which have been expressed. It has fluctuated in a very singular manner; but on one point it has not altered. In the first edition of his 'Life of Jesus,' and in the sixth volume of his 'Origins of Christianity,' he confesses himself greatly struck by the incidental indications of authenticity presented by the fourth Gospel. He notices the 'slight traces of precision;' the 'freshness of its reminiscences,' 'like those of old age;' the little touches of detail,—'It was the sixth hour;' 'It was night;' 'The man's name was Malchus;' 'They had made a fire of coals, for it was cold,' and the like. But, on the other hand, he cannot endure the discourses which are attributed to our Lord in that Gospel. He calls them 'prolix,' 'arid,' 'interminable,' 'full of abstruse metaphysics and personal allegations.' He is thus divided between the conviction, on the one hand, of the authenticity of the Gospel which is forced on him by the narrative portions of it, and the doubts of its authenticity, on the other hand, which arise from his inability to appreciate the discourses of our Saviour. Between these opposing influences he has oscillated, now regarding the Gospel as substantially the work of St. John, although edited and retouched by his disciples, and again supposing that it was not the work of St. John, but of one of his disciples, the discourses being factitious, but the narrative parts, including precious traditions, being due to St. John. His final conclusion, in his sixth volume, embodies these contradictions in their most remarkable form. 'The fourth Gospel,' we are told, 'though a writing of no value for the purpose of knowing how Jesus spoke, is superior to the other three in respect to matters of fact.'* Could there be a more extraordinary phenomenon than this—a work which possesses in the highest degree the value of an eye-witness's report on the deeds of the person of whom it speaks, but which is of no value at all in respect to his words?

But, again, what I am mainly concerned to point out is the broad fact that even hostile criticism is compelled to make these admissions; and it is particularly interesting to observe that the Gospel of St. John has baffled continually even the most reckless critics by its vivid internal marks of genuineness. There is a candour about German criticism which often redeems some of its worst faults; and the history of its opinions on this subject betrays a vacillation not less remarkable than that

* *L'Eglise Chrétienne*, 1879, pp. 58, 50. Cf. an article by M. Godet in the *Revue Chrétienne* for 1880, p. 129.

of M. Renan. The most remarkable illustration of all, perhaps, is furnished by Strauss himself. He started from the assumption of the unauthenticity of St. John's Gospel; and in point of fact, his whole attempt to resolve the Gospel history into a myth would have been condemned beforehand, if that Gospel were really the work of an Apostle. Nevertheless, in the preface to the third edition of his 'Life of Jesus,' he makes the confession that, under a renewed study of the Fourth Gospel, his early doubts of its authenticity and credibility had themselves become doubtful to him. At that point in his career, after writing his notorious book on the supposition of the Gospel of St. John not being authentic, he begins to think it may be, after all; but he returns at length to his old mind, and doubts once more the doubts he had entertained of his original doubts.* So, again, one of the ablest and most candid, as well as most learned, of Church historians in Germany, whose manual on the Life of our Lord has been a text-book in that country for fifty years, Dr. Karl Hase, after maintaining all his life the authenticity of the Gospel, surrenders it in a larger work on the same subject published in 1875, but adds that after all he does not feel sure, and thinks it very possible that the old opinion will again pre-

* See a very interesting account of the controversy on this subject in Dr. Karl Hase's *Geschichte Jesu*, 1876, pp. 26–55; especially p. 32.

vail.* The practical conclusion to be drawn from all this fluctuation seems not sufficiently attended to. That conclusion is, that it is a pure illusion to suppose that there is any general agreement of critical authority against the authenticity of the four documents on which the faith of the Church respecting the life and work of our Lord reposes. On the contrary, the assault has from first to last been a wavering one, even under the most daring leaders; and the main positions for which a Christian writer cares to contend are now practically surrendered by the most prominent of our antagonists.

In view of these considerations, we seem to be justified in dismissing once for all any doubts as to the fact that the Gospels may be substantially accepted for what they profess to be, and for what the Church has hitherto regarded them—memoirs of our Lord's life and ministry, written by men who either were eye-witnesses, or who, like St. Luke, had had perfect understanding of all things from the very first. The only question which remains, therefore, is that of the credibility of these eye-witnesses and contemporary writers. Can we rely on their accounts of the events which they had seen and heard, as being truthful, and uncoloured by superstitious imaginations? Now, I do not suppose that any serious enquirer doubts the truthfulness in point of

* *Geschichte Jesu*, p. 52.

intention of the writers of the four Gospels. It is enough to say on that point that they were disciples in the greatest school of Truth the world has ever seen. Whatever else may be thought of them, there is no question that they record, in page after page, moral teaching which brings the fiercest light of Divine truthfulness to bear on the very springs and recesses of the heart. The discourses of our Lord recorded by them correspond pre-eminently to that description of the Word of God, that it is 'quick, and powerful, and sharper than any two-edged sword, piercing even to the dividing asunder of soul and spirit, and of the joints and marrow, and is a discerner of the thoughts and intents of the heart.' Men who wrote with the consciousness of that fiery sword suspended, as it were, over their heads, cannot but have been incapable of any conscious untruthfulness.

The force of this consideration receives a striking illustration in some remarks by M. Renan, in his final review of the problem presented by the Gospel of St. John, in the appendix to the ultimate edition of his 'Life' of our Lord. His tact and candour in dealing with purely historical difficulties are often in striking contrast to his treatment of moral problems, and nowhere is this contrast more remarkable than in his summary, in the passage referred to, of the evidence respecting the authorship of the fourth Gospel. But the point to which

I would specially call attention for our present purpose is the following: M. Renan fully admits that we have to choose between acknowledging that this Gospel was really written by St. John, and alleging that it was a deliberate fraud. We must choose, he says, between two alternatives—'either the author of the fourth Gospel is a disciple of Jesus, an intimate disciple, and attached to him from the earliest moment; or else the author has employed, for the purpose of giving himself authority, an artifice which has been followed from the beginning of the book to the end, and which was designed to make it believed that he was a witness in the best position possible for reporting the truth of the events.'

'Who,' asks M. Renan, 'is the disciple of whose authority the author thus designs to avail himself? The title tells us: it is "John." There is not the slightest reason to suppose that this title was added contrary to the intentions of the real author. . . . We must therefore choose between two hypotheses: —either to recognize John, the son of Zebedee, as the author of the fourth Gospel, or to regard this Gospel as an apocryphal writing composed by some one who wished to pass it off as the work of John, the son of Zebedee. In a word, this is not a question of legends, the work of the multitude, for which no one in particular is responsible. A man who, in order to give credence to what he narrates, deceives the public not only with respect to his name, but still more with respect to the value of his witness, is not a writer of legends; he is a forger . . . This falsification, moreover, is not the only one which the author would on this supposition have committed. We have three Epistles, which likewise bear the name of John. If there is anything probable in criticism it is that the first at least of these Epistles is by the same author as the fourth Gospel. One might almost call it a chapter detached from the Gospel. . . . The author of this Epistle, like the author of the Gospel, offers himself as an eye-witness (1 John i. 1 sq.; iv. 14) of the evangelical history. He presents himself as a man well known, and enjoying high consideration in the Church.' M. Renan himself concludes: 'At the first view, it seems that the most natural hypothesis is to admit that all these writings are really the work of John, the son of Zebedee.' *

The most natural hypothesis! An appeal may confidently be made to common sense and common feeling whether, on the basis of the facts thus stated by M. Renan, any other hypothesis would not be in the highest degree unnatural and intolerable. Unless the fourth Gospel and the First Epistle of John were really written by the Apostle who bore that name, then whoever wrote them was a forger and a liar! These—to repeat an observation already made

* *Vie de Jésus*, 15th edition, pp. 537-9.

—are not my words. They are the admissions, and the very expressions of the most famous sceptic of our day. But can any conceivable difficulties of criticism, any contrast, for instance, between the literary style of the Apocalypse and of the fourth Gospel, be compared to the moral difficulty which is here stated with such candour and force? To those, perhaps, who can persuade themselves with M. Renan that the discourses of our Lord in the fourth Gospel are 'dry,' 'metaphysical,' 'flat and impossible,' such a difficulty may not appear so enormous. But as long as, by the wisdom of our reformers, those discourses are read and re-read, year by year, in the ears of English Christians, any such judgment on them will but serve to disable fatally the moral apprehension of the critic by whom it is pronounced. You know that there are no portions of the Scriptures which go more directly to your hearts, which appeal with such combined tenderness, truth, and force, to your innermost sympathies and your truest convictions. There may be much in them which is above your comprehension; but you are none the less sensible that, when listening to them, you are breathing an atmosphere of the purest simplicity and veracity, and you are forced to pay homage to the claim of the speaker when He says 'I am the truth.' But, at any rate, there can surely be no difference of opinion respecting the spirit which

animates the First Epistle of St. John. 'This is
the message which we have heard of Him and declare unto you, that God is light, and in Him is no
darkness at all. If we say that we have fellowship
with Him, and walk in darkness, we lie and do not
the truth.' 'He that saith, I know Him, and
keepeth not His commandments, is a liar, and the
truth is not in him.' Is it morally conceivable that
the man who wrote such sentences as these was
capable of the deliberate and elaborate fraud of
writing a Gospel, implying 'I knew Him' on every
page, when the whole work was a forgery and the
suggestion a lie? If there are any writings in the
world which bear the stamp of the intense truthfulness of the author, they are the First Epistle of
St. John and the fourth Gospel; and when a critic
like M. Renan is forced to admit that they must
either be the work of the Apostle or the work of
a forger, our moral sense may well be revolted at
being asked to choose between such alternatives.

But allowing that the authors of our Four
Gospels were incapable of untruth, were they
capable of hallucination? That, no doubt, is a
possibility which it is necessary to take into account. But here, again, the answer may well be
similar to that offered to the last objection. Not
only were these men disciples in the greatest school
of truthfulness the world has ever seen; they were

disciples not less in the school of the sternest realities the world has ever seen. At the risk, and in many cases at the actual cost, of a death like that of their Master, a death of torture and of ignominy, they declared themselves to be in possession of the secret of salvation for the world, of truths by which mankind might be regenerated; and they proclaimed themselves the servants of a Lord who was destined to rule the hearts of men. If any beliefs would have seemed more like hallucination than any other to the men of that day, it would have been these cardinal elements in the belief of the Evangelists and Apostles. St. Paul's message was equal foolishness in the eye of a Jew and of a Greek. To a Jew it seemed incredible that the Gentiles should become heirs of all the spiritual education of his forefathers; to the Greek or Roman it seemed a ridiculous conception that he should submit his wisdom, his art, and his power to the authority of a crucified Jew. These, as I have said, might have seemed hallucinations, if you will. But these very beliefs, the most incredible of all at that time, we know to have been founded in truth, and we see the verification of them before our eyes. The two Apostles in whose daily company St. Luke and St. Mark lived, and the other two Evangelists, St. Matthew and St. John, have laid down the moral principles on which the whole fabric of the highest civilized society now reposes, and in which every thoughtful man sees the germs and the guarantee of the future progress of our race.

Now consider to what this amounts. It shows that wherever we are able to put to the proof, not merely the truthfulness, but the sobriety, the practical insight, the moral and spiritual penetration, of the Evangelists and Apostles, their possession of these qualities is vindicated by experience on the largest possible scale. In these Gospels and Epistles a sun suddenly appeared in the spiritual heaven of mankind, which eclipsed, by the intensity of its illumination, all lesser lights in the moral firmament. This is the phenomenon which places the testimony of the Evangelists and Apostles on so different a footing from that of any other evidence to events at all similar in character. To quote instances of legends attaching to the origin of other religions is beside the mark, until an instance can be produced of such legends being associated as in this case with supreme truth, wisdom, purity, and goodness. Putting out of sight for the moment the question of miracles, there appears a general agreement of the most thoughtful men of all schools that there is not one sentiment, or even one word, for which the Evangelists or their Master are responsible which does not harmonize with the highest conceivable ideals of all that is good and true. Now, would not such uniform and ideal perfection be itself a miracle of the most perplexing and distressing kind, if it were combined with the hallucination which is attributed to the Evangelists by rationalistic criticism?

Let it be acknowledged, by all means, that we do need evidence of the most overwhelming and irrefragable character to establish the credibility of the Gospel records; as, for instance, of those narratives of the birth of our Lord to which in the next Lecture I will make some special reference. They are indeed stupendous events, out of the range of all known experience—by no means indeed inconceivable, for one of the objections against them is that the human mind has conceived and imagined such occurrences again and again—but not to be credited without the highest possible moral evidence. Hume's famous test seems by no means an unfair one for such cases. To establish a miracle, the testimony should be of such a kind that its falsehood would be more miraculous than the fact which it endeavours to establish. At all events, we need not as Christians shrink from the application of that test. To suppose that writers who declared with the utmost simplicity, clearness, and force the profoundest truths of our moral nature, and who staked their lives on the fulfilment, against all likelihood, and by the mere operation of moral and spiritual forces, of the mightiest of all revolutions in human history, whose declarations are true wherever we have been able to test them—to suppose that men who, if I may so express it, had stood at the very centre of the human universe, who saw the law of gravitation of the whole spiritual system, and determined, centuries beforehand, the orbits in which its chief planets would roll—that such men should have been visionaries and enthusiasts, capable of hallucinations about occurrences which were indissolubly bound up with the truths they proclaimed—this would be worse than miraculous; it would be monstrous.

Accordingly, when all is said, the question of the credibility of the Gospels will be found to turn, in the main, upon internal evidence. They are their own best witnesses. It is the conspicuous and intense veracity of their authors which has chiefly maintained their authority through the controversies of eighteen centuries, and which maintains them still. It is this which gives them so firm a hold upon the hearts of believers, and by which all the difficulties raised by criticism are ultimately shattered. Such evidence as we have been dwelling on may not, indeed, be formally demonstrative. In that respect it shares the character of almost all historical and literary evidence. But it will ever be convincing to those who recognize the supreme moral and spiritual force inherent in our Lord's words, and in the records of the Evangelists. As we have seen, the objections raised against the authenticity of a Gospel like that of St. John depend, in the ultimate resort, on the question whether the discourses of our Lord in that Gospel are pregnant with moral and spiritual truth, or are arid and metaphysical. A man whose moral sense is closed to their force cannot be convinced by any amount of evidence that the Gospel, as a whole, is the work of an Apostle. But in proportion as those words enter your hearts and pierce them like a two-edged sword, in proportion as the moral force of the Gospels overpowers your whole nature, will you be prepared to give due weight to the other elements in their testimony, and will you be disposed to think that the most incredible of all things would be that they should not be literally true.

LECTURE III

THE BIRTH OF OUR LORD

"Now the birth of Jesus Christ was on this wise: When as His mother Mary was espoused to Joseph, before they came together, she was found with child of the Holy Ghost."—*Matthew* i. 18.

It has now been shown that we stand on firm ground in accepting the narratives of the Four Gospels as faithful records of the life and ministry of our Lord; that they contain, at least in all substantial points, the direct testimony of two eye-witnesses, and the reports of two other persons who were in direct and intimate communication with eye-witnesses. We have further seen how immense is the presumption in favour alike of the truthfulness of the Evangelists and of their soundness of judgment, afforded on the one hand by the profound love of truth which they display, and on the other hand by the verification which experience has afforded of their insight into the great realities of man's moral nature and of the course of history. When they thus command our confidence on all the more central and weighty matters of their testimony, it is natural to conclude that they must equally deserve it in details; and we shall at least be prepared to hold our judgment in suspense in respect to minor difficulties in their narratives.

These considerations must be carefully borne in mind in passing to-day to consider in their order the cardinal facts in our Lord's ministry, as enumerated in St. Peter's address to Cornelius and in the Creed of the Church. But we must needs commence by observing that, from the point of view we have gained, we are enabled, or rather compelled, to put aside at once the principal speculations of late years respecting our Lord's method and purpose. For all those speculations proceed on the re-arrangement, according to the views of the particular writer, of the records of the Gospels; one part being taken out and another left, and the whole being readjusted to meet the author's comprehension of the case. One writer proposes to discuss our Lord's object and scheme without reference to His theology, as though the deepest and most characteristic of His motives could possibly be excluded from His work. Another endeavours to exclude His miracles altogether from consideration, and a third resolves them into a half-conscious, half-unconscious illusion. M. Renan, who, as we have seen, accepts the four Gospels as 'serious documents,' providing for us, to a great extent, the evidence of eye-witnesses, nevertheless constructs a story of our Lord's life in flagrant contradiction with the main order of events as uniformly narrated by these witnesses. The Gospels place the commencement of our Lord's ministry at His baptism by John, and exhibit Him from that time forward as preaching the Gospel of the Kingdom, and working miracles in accordance with it. But M. Renan imagines out of his own mind a kind of idyllic period in Galilee before our Lord's communication with John, during which He was wholly occupied with what that writer is pleased to consider the purely moral instruction of the Sermon on the Mount. It seems enough to say that any method which deals in this arbitrary manner with the unanimous testimony of serious witnesses is self-condemned.

It must be added that there is a presumption very difficult to comprehend in the tone of mind which assumes a capacity for sitting in judgment, as it were, on the work of our Lord, and measuring His aims by its own standard. On any supposition, His moral and spiritual power has been, and still remains, superior to the conceptions and ideals of all other men. It is only reasonable to suppose, therefore, that it must in numerous points be wholly above and beyond our comprehension. So far as we have definite statements preserved to us, such as we believe we possess in the Gospels, we may hope in some measure to apprehend it. But if we cannot trust the order of their narration, we are simply in presence of a mysterious manifestation of superhuman wisdom, goodness, and power, which we cannot hope to explain. It is not surprising, therefore, that every writer on this subject who departs from the records of the Gospel and the faith of the Church, develops some new scheme inconsistent with those of his predecessors. The Church alone has been consistent from the first in its acceptance, and in its general interpretation, of the story in the Gospels; and the fact that this uniform impression should have been produced by the four Gospels upon all who have submitted themselves simply to their instruction, must alone raise a great presumption in favour of its harmony with the real truth of the case.

Now these are the considerations from which we have to start in considering the credibility of such a passage in the Gospel history as that of the miraculous birth of our Lord, with the angelic messages which accompanied it. The information could of course only be derived from one source, namely, from the Mother of our Lord herself; and as to the possibility of Apostles and Apostolic men receiving this information, it is enough to know that, after the Ascension as St. Luke states, the Apostles 'continued with one accord in prayer and supplication, with the women, and Mary the mother of Jesus, and with His brethren.' We know nothing of Mary's life after this; but our Lord on the Cross commended her to the care of St. John, and the solemn charge was doubtless fulfilled. It follows, therefore, that for a whole generation after the compilation of the first three Gospels —according to the admissions already quoted—that very Apostle was still living who was better able than any other man to know whether the accounts of our Lord's birth given by St. Luke and St. Matthew were in accord with Mary's testimony. The objectors to the truth of the record have most strangely laid stress on the fact that the narrative is not repeated by St. John. This is but an extreme instance of a most unreasonable assumption constantly employed by rationalistic critics—namely, that because an Evangelist does not mention some important fact, he was ignorant of it, or disbelieved it. In this case St. John, by the supposition, was writing at least thirty years after the narrative had been placed on record by St. Matthew and St. Luke. His Gospel is throughout, to a large extent, supplementary to theirs, omitting many things which they had reported, and adding many which they did not report. In accordance with this general characteristic, it is perfectly natural that he should not mention occurrences which were sufficiently narrated already, and were accepted by the whole Christian Church of his day. The really significant fact is that, knowing, as it is admitted he must have known, that such a narrative was in circulation, he says not one word to deprecate belief in it; but, on the contrary, insists on the central truth of which it was the outward form and expression—that 'the Word was made flesh.' Mary herself comes before us, throughout the New Testament narrative, as a singularly quiet, thoughtful, humble, retiring figure, pondering things in her heart and silently treasuring them, free from all excitement and eagerness. John is the very Apostle —if a distinction may be made between them—of light and truth: his message was, that God is light, and in Him is no darkness at all; and that if we walk in the light, as He is in the light, we have fellowship one with another. It is impossible to suppose that anything approaching to a pious fraud would have found countenance from two such simple natures; and we seem therefore to possess, on the critical suppositions already assumed, a singularly direct personal testimony to the truth of the narratives in question.

In the time available for these Lectures, it would be impracticable to enter into all the difficulties which have been raised respecting details in the two narratives of St. Matthew and St. Luke. I shall venture to say summarily, that the historical difficulties connected with such matters as the Census of Cyrenius have been more than sufficiently met, and to refer for that part of the argument to the 'Speaker's Commentary.' I do not say that in every detail the variations in the accounts have been completely harmonized. In some few points there is room for a difference of opinion respecting the true explanation. But it is quite unreasonable to expect that in such brief narratives the sequence of events should always be perspicuous; and it may be added, as a general principle, that while the Evangelists are always in harmony in the main points of any narrative, there are slight differences between them, which prove that their narrations were in great measure independent; that their records, in fact, are marked by the same minor variations which are generally to be observed in accounts of the same event given by independent witnesses—variations which, in other matters, are always held to be an additional guarantee of trustworthiness, so long as they stop short of being contradictions. The title on the Cross is a familiar instance of this variation; but an example perhaps still more instructive may be found in the narrative of the feeding of the five thousand, contained in the 14th chapter of St. Matthew, the 6th of St. Mark, the 9th of St. Luke, and the 6th of St. John. This is the only miracle of which an account is preserved to us by all four Evangelists;

and a comparison of the narratives will show that, while perfectly consistent in the essential facts, there are details peculiar to each. For example, in the first three Gospels, our Lord says to His disciples in general, 'Give ye them to eat;' while in St. John He addresses an enquiry especially to Philip: 'Whence shall we buy bread that these may eat?' But notwithstanding this, the main facts of the story are narrated by the four Evangelists in almost the same words.

While, however, thus deprecating the demand for an absolutely identical narrative, it may be well to observe that there is no point in the Gospel history on which the narratives are more completely harmonious in respect to the essential facts of the case than in regard to our Lord's birth. Thus, it may seem, at first sight, a formidable objection against the occurrence of the marvellous events attending the Saviour's birth, that they seem to have been unknown at Nazareth; that in the subsequent history there is no indication that the neighbours of Joseph and Mary were at all aware of there having been anything unusual in the time and other circumstances of their Child's birth; and again, that the visit of the wise men and the incidents connected with it seem to have been so entirely forgotten. Now, if the birth had occurred at Nazareth, and if no break had interrupted the course of the life of Joseph and Mary and of our Lord, between the time when all Jerusalem was disturbed at the reported birth of a king of the Jews, and the days when our Lord began to be about thirty years of age, 'being, as was supposed, the son of Joseph,' these objections might have some weight. But, in point of fact, St. Matthew tells us of events which afford a perfectly simple and natural explanation of everything. We are told that our Lord was born, not at Nazareth, but at Bethlehem; and that after His birth, before the return of His parents to the former city, there intervened the slaughter of the children at Bethlehem, and the flight into Egypt. There did thus exist the very break which is requisite to explain the ignorance of the people of Nazareth respecting the circumstances in question.

In all other respects, the alleged supernatural birth must be admitted to be at least in harmony with other unquestioned facts. It seemed fairer and more simple, for the purpose of these Lectures, to treat first the subject which presented itself earliest in chronological order, and in the recital of the Creed. But we should have been pursuing a course in some respects more natural in itself, and more in harmony with our Lord's own method, if we had deferred the consideration of this subject until we were prepared to estimate its probability in the light thrown upon it by our Lord's subsequent life and work. It has often been asked why, if our Lord could have referred to this supernatural origin, if His mother could have borne witness to it, if He were really the Son of David born under miraculous circumstances at Bethlehem, He should have allowed, as He more than once did in the course of the history, objections to remain unanswered, which would at once have been removed by an establishment of these facts? The answer may well be that the facts, from their essentially private and delicate character, could never have been established to the satisfaction of persons who were not predisposed to believe them by the conviction, based on other grounds, of our Lord's divine, or at least superhuman, character. The calumnies afterwards circulated on the subject are alone sufficient justification of the reticence which our Lord observed on this subject in the presence of hostile or unbelieving crowds. On such a topic the principle is eminently applicable: 'If they believe not Moses and the prophets, neither will they be persuaded though one rose from the dead.' If men rejected His moral and spiritual claims, He refused to show them signs from heaven; and still more sacred considerations must have debarred Him from appealing to His mother to answer their cavils.

Similar reasons may account for the absence of the

narrative from St. Mark, if that be, as there is good reason to think, the earliest Gospel. At all events, it would be natural that the miraculous birth of our Lord should not be put in the fore-front of the first proclamation of the Gospel. It would most fitly be taught, as it is narrated by St. Luke, to those who were already believers, 'that they might know the certainty of those things wherein they had been instructed,' but it would be protected by reserve from the misapprehensions of unbelievers. To a great extent, the case is the same in the present day. The full force of the reasons for accepting the narratives of our Lord's birth can only be perceived by arguing back from the resurrection. It at least seems a conclusive answer to objections on the mere score of the miraculous character of the birth, to say that if our Lord was not like other men in His death, it is probable, rather than otherwise, that He was unlike them in the commencement of His life. But without assuming this point, it may be sufficient to call attention to another consideration. It is to be borne in mind that in His character, at all events, our Lord so surpassed all other men who have ever appeared on earth as to be distinguished from them, not only in degree, but in His very nature. There is something absolutely unique in His whole character, and if this fact be unquestionable, what more natural than that there should be something unique in His origin?

There is perhaps no point of our Christian Creed on which it is more important to dwell at the present day. It is indeed the primary truth of that Creed at all times, but there are circumstances characteristic of our own day which give it an exceptional prominence. It is, perhaps, the principle on which the Gospel is most directly at issue with the ideas which have been acquiring increasing influence throughout this century. In different ways, both at home and abroad, the minds of men have become penetrated with the conception of development or of evolution, until it has become peculiarly unwelcome to them to accept in any form the notion of a break, or a new commencement, in human life, whether in the past, or in the present. The history of this growth of thought reaches back to the beginning of the century, to the German philosophy which then became prominent—that of Hegel; and the doctrine of physical evolution, which has of late years attracted such adherence among ourselves, is but one application of this idea. It was applied in Germany to human nature, before it was worked out in reference to physical nature in this country, and its disastrous consequences have been felt in numerous directions throughout the whole field of theology and criticism. Its cardinal principle is that all history is but the development of ideas and tendencies inherent in human nature—human nature in the strict sense of the word, a nature not influenced nor disturbed in its regular evolution by any alien or supernatural forces. Whatever manifestation of human thought or belief is recorded in history must be traced, according to this philosophy, to antecedents in human nature itself, to causes which we can discover and follow out, just as we can trace all physical effects to physical causes. Christianity therefore must be accounted for by the natural working of the influences which had preceded it. There must be evidence that it was produced by the natural development of religious impulses which had been maturing among the Jews, combined after a while with similar influences of Greek philosophy and Roman life. The Origins of Christianity—to use the phrase which the eminent French sceptic has adopted and made familiar—must thus be perceptible in the ordinary workings of the human heart, amidst the circumstances by which men were surrounded in the first century, just as the rise of Buddhism and Mahometanism can be explained by a knowledge of the social and religious conditions of the people among whom they were first proclaimed.

But it soon became obvious that this was not sufficient. If Christianity was thus to be explained as a mere natural development, the product of the influences of its day, a further step, however momentous, was inevitable. Christ Himself must be thus explained. If He was a supernatural Being, bringing a new creative force into the world, the whole of this theory of the Origins of Christianity fell to the ground; and accordingly those who applied this philosophy in Germany were in a very short time driven by their principles to the most desperate efforts to explain the whole Gospel history on natural grounds and by natural causes. The very idea of miracles was antagonistic to the central thought of such a philosophy, and the miraculous occurrences narrated in the Gospels had thus by some means to be explained away. Above all was this the case with the primary miracle, that of the Incarnation. Men disguised the momentous conclusion from themselves for a while; but there was no escape from it, and the Germans, with their characteristic audacity, faced it fifty years ago. All ordinary rationalistic explanations failed, one after another; and at last Strauss, the boldest of the German critics, declared the whole Gospel History to be mythical, and the mere embodiment in the form of myths of the ideas of the age. This was carried one step further, and a similar attack was made on the Apostolic Histories by Baur and his followers. Thus one of the leading authorities of our day on philosophical questions in Germany, originally a disciple of Hegel, says that ' the Hegelian philosophy was not only in harmony with Baur's interpretation of history, but exerted an influence on it through the idea of the development of humanity, as determined by an inner necessity, proceeding by an immanent dialectic, and manifesting in accordance with a fixed law all the elements which are included in the nature of Spirit.' *

This, it cannot be too clearly borne in mind, is the key to the whole critical assault of this century on the authority and credibility of the Scripture History, whether of the Old or of the New Testament. It has not, in any instance, been prompted by an impartial and independent study of the facts for themselves. The critical difficulties did not make the philosophy. The philosophy has made the critical difficulties. Men have allowed their minds, in the Apostle's language, to be made spoil of by a vain philosophy, which assumed that no influence had ever operated on human nature above human nature itself; and then, when they were confronted with the momentous facts of the Christian Creed and the Christian Scriptures, they set themselves with desperate efforts to explain away their credibility, to transform their records, and to find

---

* Quoted in Ueberweg's ' *Geschichte der Philosophie*,' 5th ed., Berlin, 1880; part iii. p. 365.

excuses of whatever kind for evading their evidence. After being applied to the Gospel History and the Apostolic records, an attempt is now being made to apply this philosophy to the Old Testament, and to represent the faith of the Jews, not as the result of a supernatural education by the miraculous interposition of God, but as the mere natural development of Semitic tendencies. The attempt has failed with respect to the New Testament, and has resulted in the critical defeat of each successive school in Germany; and a similar defeat may safely be predicted for this new application of the philosophy of the century.

It was, however, it will be seen, a true instinct which urged those who were possessed by these views to make so determined an assault on the great facts and records of the Gospel; for those facts establish in the sphere of human history and human life a truth which is in diametrical antagonism with any such conception of human development. Certainly, a place is found in the revelation of the Gospel and in the Christian Creed for the facts of life which are exaggerated in this philosophy. The Scripture fully recognizes and teaches that there has been a development in human affairs, a gradual evolution, if any one prefers to use the word, of moral, intellectual, and spiritual life. Our Saviour is declared to have come in the fulness of time, when the Divine education of Jew and Greek alike had been brought to the point at which they were fitted to receive a new revelation, and to be subject to a new creative influence. The long centuries of Jewish and heathen history had been working, under the Divine hand, towards that critical moment, and the ground had been laboriously prepared to receive the seed. But allowing for this, that which the Scriptures declare is that there was, in fact, a seed—that a new germ of life was sown in the field of human nature, and that when the fulness of time was come, God sent forth His Son to be the source of a new creation. The creative process was similar to that which is described in the book of Genesis. God formed man of the dust of the ground, and breathed into his nostrils the breath of life, and man became a living soul. It may be, for all that directly concerns the Christian faith, that the dust of the ground has been gradually developed through successive forms of animal life, until a frame has been evolved capable of becoming the instrument of the human spirit; but the frame did not evolve that spirit. It was necessary for God to breathe into it the breath of life by a new creative act. It will be understood that I am not here entering on the general question of the truth of the peculiar doctrine of evolution as applied to physical nature. Such considerations as have passed before us may, indeed, well raise a presumption in our minds on that subject. But all we are now concerned to observe is that human nature is exempted from that principle in the experiences, the history, the hopes, which are the most precious to it. The Gospel, in its proclamation of the Incarnation of our Lord, in the history of His ministry, and in its application to ourselves, reveals a principle entirely independent of natural human development. A new creation arises when our Lord was born. A second Adam, the Lord from heaven, descended into the midst of the old creation, and began to regenerate it by a new spiritual and Divine influence. A spiritual and real regeneration commenced ; human souls were privileged to be born again, 'not of corruptible seed but of incorruptible, by the word of God which liveth and abideth for ever.' The Christian church is not a product of human nature ; it is the construction of the Spirit of God, working upon human nature from above, and renewing it after the image of the Creator. These are the momentous and precious realities which are indissolubly bound up with the mysterious truth of our Lord's Incarnation.

As has just been implied, they are not less momentous to our own spiritual life than to our view of the great truths of the Christian Creed. The general tendency of which I have spoken is liable to exert a very dangerous influence over our personal life. It tends of necessity to obscure to our minds the blessed truth of our being ourselves the subjects of this regenerating and transforming influence—capable, as St. Paul says, of being 're-newed in the spirit of our mind' (Eph. iv. 23). One of the most important of all the questions we can put to ourselves respecting our own moral and spiritual life is, whether we, in our own souls, are the mere subjects of a process of development and evolution. Are we intended to be, do we allow ourselves to be, the mere product of the various forces, good or bad, which are brought to bear upon us in the visible world of our fellows, whether by our family associations or by our age, and are we conformed to this world around us? or do we recognize that we have within us a divine spiritual power, by means of which we may be 'transformed by the renewing of our mind'? Here again, as in the larger view of the subject, there is ample scope for the legitimate recognition of the natural education to which we are subjected by the circumstances amidst which we live. The growth of each individual soul is governed by the hand of God in a similar manner to that in which He guided the education of the world before our Lord came. The circumstances of our lives, the various influences which His providence has brought to bear upon us, are all being directed to plough and prepare the soil of our hearts for His word to take root in us; and it behoves us to cherish with the utmost care every gracious providence of this kind. The Gospel, in proclaiming the presence and operation of miraculous influences, never disregards or disparages those which are natural. Every miracle is practically accompanied by the command, 'Gather up the fragments, that nothing be lost.' No man is justified in depending on divine aid if he neglects those fragments of opportunity, afforded him by the natural providence of God. But none the less it is our supreme blessing to be assured that we are not dependent solely on such natural influences, and on our natural power to turn them to account. The Spirit of God is bestowed upon us, to regenerate our weak and corrupt natures, to give to our own efforts a power they could not have exerted of themselves, and gradually to create us afresh in the image of the Saviour.

Nothing less could be an adequate satisfaction to any human spirit which is conscious of its intense imperfection and corruption. Which of us could bear to look forward to an eternity in which we should be surrounded by our present infirmities? Or who that has struggled with earnestness against his besetting sins but must feel his need of some regenerating grace? The promise of such grace is our great blessing for the present, and our supreme hope for the future. It is the privilege of the

Christian that, in proportion to his faithful efforts and prayers, a new man is gradually formed within him, which brings his old nature into ever increasing subjection, and which will hereafter completely transform him. To this hope he looks forward amidst the decay of his natural frame. 'If our earthly house of this tabernacle be dissolved, we have a building of God, an house not made with hands, eternal in the heavens.' The Saviour's supernatural birth, no less than His resurrection, is a pledge to him of this possibility; and thus he is taught by the Church to pray: 'Almighty God, who hast given us Thy only begotten Son to take our nature upon him, and to be born of a pure Virgin; Grant that we being regenerate, and made Thy children by adoption and grace, may daily be renewed by Thy Holy Spirit; through the same our Lord Jesus Christ.'

LECTURE IV

THE NAME OF JESUS

"Thou shalt call His name JESUS, for He shall save His people from their sins."—*Matt.* i. 21.

These words seem to embody the very substance of the work and office of our Lord, as it appeared to the eye of the inhabitants of heaven. Angels were His heralds when He came into the world, and on each occasion when these voices from heaven were heard, they were directed to this one point. When the angel Gabriel appeared to Mary, he said, 'Thou shalt bring forth a son, and shalt call His name Jesus.' When the angel appeared to Joseph, he announced the same name, and gave the assurance of the text; and after our Lord's birth, when the angels appeared to the shepherds, and the glory of the Lord shone round about them, the celestial proclamation was, 'Fear not: for, behold, I bring you good tidings of great joy, which shall be to all people. For unto you is born this day, in the city of David, a Saviour, which is Christ the Lord.' To the wondering gaze of heaven, the one grand fact

THE NAME OF JESUS

to be realized, in the event they were announcing and celebrating, was that a Saviour had come into the world, one so called because He should save His people from their sins. This thought overpowers all others, and sums up in itself the whole glorious announcement which Heaven desired to proclaim to earth.

We may therefore meditate upon this text as one which conveys the whole message of the Gospel. We have in our Bibles the Gospel according to St. Matthew, the Gospel according to St. Mark, the Gospel according to St. Luke, and the Gospel according to St. John; that is to say, we have the one Gospel of Jesus Christ, expressed in the four various forms in which those Evangelists delivered it. Similarly, the message of the text may be regarded as the Gospel, and the whole Gospel, according to those angelic messengers who were commissioned to announce it to earth. We may be sure, therefore, that these short and simple words express the cardinal truth of the Christian dispensation, and that we ought to make them the centre of our whole view of life, and of the revelation vouchsafed to us in the Gospel. At a time like the present, when the busy and anxious speculations of the day are discussing the problems of life and of Christianity from such varying points of view, and when such ever-shifting solutions of those problems are offered to us, it is more than ever desirable that we should concentrate our thoughts on the truth thus unmistakably pointed out to us as the key to the whole mystery. Heaven surveys with clear and serene vision this confused and struggling scene, and its voice strikes home, in a single sentence, to the heart of the great drama of life. If we are to appreciate the moral probability and verisimilitude of the records in the four Gospels, it is necessary for us to realize the facts of human nature as they are presented by the sacred writers; and a due apprehension of the significance of the name of 'Jesus' is thus essential to any argument in defence or elucidation of the Gospels.

Consider, then, in the first place, what was the one great fact in the actual condition of mankind on which the eye of Heaven was fixed. It was that men need salvation, and that that from which they need to be saved is from their sins. The whole sum and substance of human needs, all that men crave to be delivered from, is thus represented to us as involved in the one word, sin. All else is passed over. Even the consequences of sin are not specifically mentioned, as though the consideration of them were subordinate to our apprehension of the main purpose of the Divine salvation which is announced. Sin, and sin alone, is what men need to be delivered from.

Let us ask ourselves how far our minds are in harmony with this conception of our condition. It is a conception which it proved impossible to bring home to the mass of men at the time of our Lord; and among ourselves, even when it is nominally admitted, there is reason to fear it is still most imperfectly apprehended. Men in our own day look around the world as the Jews did, and are sensible of the sufferings, the oppressions, the injustices, the confusions, which meet their view, and they crave and yearn, as they have ever done, for some salvation for themselves and their fellows. Just as the Jews were craving for some Messiah to arise, and deliver them from the hand of their enemies, by some sudden stroke of force or policy, so if we cast our eye over the Christian world at this time, we behold a very similar spectacle. We see men's attention occupied and distracted by conflicting social, political, and philosophical schemes— one philosophy after another, one political dream after another, absorbing their interests, and holding out to them, as they fondly believe, the promise of a better future. Some of these philosophical and social schemes may have their place and function in the development of thought and of society; and so far as they can be kept in their place, they are not to be disparaged. But they are all imperfect, when considered from the point of view on which the text insists. They fail to recognize that the essential weakness of human nature lies where it is indicated by the angelic message. They all begin with something else besides men's sins, with some circumstances more or less external to the secret life of their moral nature—it may be with their political or social condition, or even with their physical constitution. They do not recognize, like the Gospel, and like the Bible from first to last, that moral evil is the one central source of all evil, and that towards overcoming this the main efforts of a Saviour of mankind ought to be concentrated.

We may appreciate this the more clearly if we briefly call to mind the state of the world at the time these words were uttered, for we shall find our own position but little altered in its essential characteristics. This angelic message certainly offered a strange contrast to the predominant thoughts and feelings of the world at that day. The wonderful empire of Rome, which was destined to supply some of the most important elements of all future civilization, was gradually consolidating its strength; it was crushing independent nationalities like that of the Jews, dazzling and overawing men by its splendour and force. It seemed the one great fact with which men had to deal. It evidently absorbed the attention of the Jews themselves, and before long they aroused themselves to a deadly grapple with it. At that moment, and amidst this wonderful development of organized force and law, a voice from heaven is heard, and a Divine message announces the advent of the King and Saviour of mankind. And to what does it address itself? It passes by all the external interests with which the Jews were busying and perplexing themselves; it leaves them all, as it were, to take care of themselves, and it proclaims that the coming Saviour has but one thing to do—to save His people from their sins. All the rest could be left to follow naturally from this one deliverance; but here was the point of vital interest in the whole strange and painful scene. It was a marvellous contrast between human and Divine judgment. But if the same voice were now heard from Heaven, would the contrast be less startling? We know too well with what excitements, what passions, what political struggles, what wars and revolutions, what domestic difficulties and sufferings, the thoughts of the world, and our own thoughts, are from day to day distracted and oppressed. Amidst it all, the Christian Church proclaims its message; and Sunday after Sunday it recalls the old voice from Heaven, which summons men above all things to repent, and to seek salvation from their sins. But how far is it realized—how far, let us ask ourselves, do we realize—that this is the interest which predominates over all others, which determines the result of every other effort of human nature, which not only decides the fate of individuals, but which exalts or abases nations, and that here alone is to be found that wisdom, by which, in the ultimate resort, kings reign and princes decree justice?

In meditating, indeed, on these words, we should do ill to forget the intimate connection which, with the Jews to whom they were first spoken, as with ourselves, unites their private, their national, and their worldwide significance. There is no reason to think that the craving of the Jews for their temporal deliverance from subjugation to a heathen power was in itself wrong or unworthy. The King of the Jews, who had led His people out of bondage in former times by His glorious arm, cannot be supposed to have been indifferent to the new bondage into which they had fallen. The feelings of His heart must still have been expressed by His own words in the Psalm, 'O that my people had hearkened unto me, for if Israel had walked in my ways, I should soon have put down their enemies, and turned my hand against their adversaries.' It is equally impossible to suppose Him indifferent to the temporal needs, sufferings, and problems which engage the attention of statesmen and philosophers in the present day. He, far more than any one among ourselves, must, in the language of the

Scriptures, be 'grieved to the heart,' by the wars and rumours of wars, the social disorder and misery, under which so great a part of the world groans, and of which large classes among ourselves have so sad a share. But what He would have us remember, as we labour to deliver ourselves and others from these evils, is that no mere social and political arrangements, no bravery and no wisdom, if it be only the wisdom of this world, will free us and other nations from these terrible scourges. The only Saviour of mankind is He who saves them from their sins, and we shall carry out His work effectually, in proportion as we follow His method. In maladies of the body, when the whole frame is shaken by some violent fever or convulsion, the real source of the mischief may be known by the physician to consist in the derangement of the minutest cells of the brain, or of the most elementary functions of the constitution. It is precisely the same with the body politic, and with the world at large. It is by disbelief in the elementary truths of religion, by unfaithfulness to the elementary dictates of morality, that the reason and the will are corrupted, and life is disorganized; and if we would solve the problems which distract us, and discern our way amidst the perplexities of life, our only sure method is to quicken our belief in these elementary truths, and to invigorate our practice of these elementary moral duties.

What a tremendous task do not these considerations set before us! But, for our encouragement, let us remember what a desperate task, to all human calculations, it must have appeared at the time this blessed assurance was uttered: the whole world, with one small exception, given over to idolatry, and philosophers and moralists conscious of their inability to cope with the vices inseparably entwined with the popular superstitions. We contemplate at the present day a vaster world; but the problems before us are not more tremendous than those which presented themselves to the eye of an early Christian. Most of us, indeed, have reason enough to be appalled, as we reflect on the evil of our own hearts, and the consequences of our own past lives. There is surely no thoughtful man who, in his serious moments, can contrast what he is with what he ought to have been, without remorse, if not dismay. Some more and some less, but all undeniably, we are conscious that the true life of our souls has been marred, that the flesh lusts against the spirit, and that we cannot do the things that we would; that sin of one kind or another is bound up in our very frame, absorbed, as it were, into the very fibres of our brain, and perpetually reasserting itself in imperious habits. To all serious souls the Church's daily Confession, with its keen self-abasement, and in their most solemn moments the still deeper confession of the Communion Service, embodies their bitter experience. We struggle and we gain ground; but to the last we must be impressed with an intense sense of imperfection, if not of wilful sin, and never in this world is our deliverance from sin complete. If we were left to contemplate men as left to themselves, and to the play of natural laws and forces, the problem presented to us by considerations such as these would surpass in its darkness and oppressiveness all others. Whole races, we know, have been oppressed through long generations by the experience and contemplation of the visible sufferings of mankind, and by the physical and temporal evils which weigh on them. But what are these, in comparison of the injury and ruin presented by our moral nature?

It is always difficult — it was difficult in the days of Socrates and Plato, and is not less difficult now — to induce men to contemplate the state of their souls with the same keenness of perception which they bestow on that of their bodies. Is it not, to say the least, too rare, for men and women to shudder and shrink from a moral defilement with the same instinctive horror with which they recoil from a loathsome disease? And are there not sins—and among them some which inflict the deepest wounds on the moral nature—

are there not blasphemies against God, and offences against one another, which are too frequently discussed, if not committed, with lightness? But the course of modern discoveries renders us more than ever justified in regarding the moral condition of mankind as analogous to their physical; and the imperfection, the disease, the weakness, and the death, which affect our physical frame, afford a visible, though but an imperfect, picture of the moral and spiritual ruin of which our souls are capable, and from which, to a fearful extent, they actually suffer. Moral maladies, moreover, are far more general than physical, and far more subtle. They may take the form even of virtues, and pervert the judgment of whole masses of men. Even virtue itself has its dangers, and persons who escape degrading forms of vice may be overtaken by vanity or self-righteousness—vices which may become, as was shown in the case of the Pharisees, not less injurious than grosser sins to the health of the moral nature. To this must be added the unquestionable fact, that vast numbers of men and women are born in circumstances which renders some form of moral disease almost a part of their nature, and that most persons inherit some special evil tendency. Contemplating such a picture of the moral condition of human nature, what an appalling problem does it not present to us! How natural—nay, from a mere worldly point of view, how reasonable—would it not be to despair if we were left to ourselves! How justifiable would be that pessimism, in which, from time to time, the bitter experience of human nature finds its sad expression!

There seems, indeed, one school of thought now among us which can contemplate the spectacle with philosophical complacency—watching simply, as it supposes, the gradual evolution of moral life on the whole, and not concerning itself with individual failures. But those failures, with all they involve, are the very miseries from which we crave to be delivered, and delivered now. It is these which are denounced and lamented in the too true confessions of pessimist philosophers. They are justly the most sensitive point in the Christian conscience; they constitute the ever-present burden of individual hearts. The question which must ever recur to us is that which—thank God!—is answered in the text. What is to bestow upon ourselves and upon our fellows the spiritual and moral health for which we each of us crave? Where is the remedy to be found which can penetrate the whole moral and spiritual world? And how are we each and all to be lifted out of our natural condition of utter imperfection and sin? A philosophy or a religion which fails to answer that question, for the relief of every individual soul, leaves unsolved the grand problem of humanity;

and with the exception of the Gospel, every religion and every philosophy has, by its own confession, thus failed—above all, that agnostic philosophy which now asserts itself so loudly among us.

I have said, however, that the question is answered in the text; and just in proportion as we realize the overwhelming oppression just described, shall we appreciate its blessed assurance. It proclaims that there is One who will save His people from their sins. It is necessary to apprehend distinctly the definite character of that announcement. It directs us to a person who, by His own work and act, will save His people. The pronoun is emphatic—$αὐτὸς$ $σώσει$—HE will save His people. The message, therefore, does not simply proclaim to those people the way of salvation, leaving them to their own exertions alone in following it. Still less is it content with announcing to them a clearer revelation of the laws of their nature. That which is announced is more than a revelation, it is a birth. It is the introduction into the world of a new creation, the second Adam, the Lord from heaven, henceforth to be present, by His personal power and Spirit, to redeem men, to regenerate them, to save them: not merely, be it observed, to teach them how to be saved, but to save them—to act with them, and for them, and in them; to be at their side in life and in death, to be Himself the propitiation for their sins with the God whom they have forgotten and offended—in a word, to die for them and to live with them, and to render it possible for them to work out their own salvation, by working with them both to will and to do of His good pleasure.

It is this revelation of a personal Saviour which constitutes the cardinal element of the Gospel message; and whether in days of controversy, or in hours of temptation and sorrow, it needs above all other things to be borne in mind. Never was it more necessary to insist on it than at the present day. In the controversies we hear around us, and from which few of us can altogether escape, the Gospel is constantly compared with other religions, and with forms of philosophy, as though the moral truths enforced by them constituted an adequate ground of comparison. Considering the question, indeed, simply on that ground, the claims of our faith are overwhelming. But it is important to remember that all discussions conducted on this level leave out of sight the main fact—the one only fact on which the heavenly messengers cared to dwell—that the Gospel proclaims the coming into the world of a living Saviour, who is Himself perpetually saving His people from their sins, and who has promised that hereafter He will completely deliver them. When we hear any principles which involve the abandonment of the Gospel discussed, so to speak, with a light heart, this simple truth and promise must surely have been left out of sight. If there be, as the Gospel says, a perfectly Holy and Almighty being, the man Jesus, in all His gentleness, all His wisdom, all His power, perpetually at our side, desiring to hear us, to guide us. to control us, to save us, what man or woman can contemplate the surrender of such an infinite blessing without an intense pang? Who would willingly forego the perpetual presence of a perfect friend? Above all things who would forego it, for time and for eternity, if that friend be a perfect Saviour? It would surely check many a crude speculation, and many a rash neglect of the claims of our faith, if men bore in mind more clearly this simple and cardinal element in it. It is not simply a truth more or less which is abandoned by unbelief, but a Person—a living and a present Saviour.

In a word, the message of the Gospel, and its essential blessing, is not merely the revelation of a truth; it is the creation of a fact—the most blessed fact in life — that every human being has a Saviour at his side, and that in proportion as he trusts that Saviour's help and follows His guidance, he will be delivered from all his evil. The methods, indeed, of that deliverance are various, and the Saviour works by natural as well as by supernatural means. The salvation of souls has been wrought by sudden miracles in Apostolic times, and since then by conversions scarcely less miraculous. At other times, and in other cases, it has been worked out by a gradual, and perhaps painful education—it may be by a severe and bitter discipline. There is sternness, as well as gentleness, in the character of a true Saviour; and as His treatment of His own people shows, He is capable of wrath as well as of mercy. As applied in daily life, that salvation involves the use of all means for moral and spiritual purification. As with our physical, so with our moral diseases, the Saviour has proved to us by His miracles that they can all be overcome, and that He possesses the power to deliver us from any evil whatever; but it would seem as though He were educating us, in both cases, to the utmost possible development of our natural resources. While, however, we are thus struggling to do our utmost with all the means at our disposal, with all the resources of religious and useful learning, with the wisdom of statesmen and with all the applications of art and science, the gracious truth is proclaimed to us that He is with us, to bless every agency that we can employ, and to complete our work and His own by the mighty operation of His spirit. We are justified by His death; and we are saved by His life. To as many as believe in

Him, He gives the power to become the sons of God, and they are assured that they will hereafter be like Him, seeing Him as He is, and reflecting His glory.

So simple, yet so far-reaching in its application, is the heavenly summary of the Gospel message. It is the life and soul of all Christian doctrine; and in proportion as it is borne in mind, does every truth of our faith become illuminated with a gracious light, at once human and Divine. Take, for instance, the doctrine of the Atonement, with which this text has sometimes, perhaps, been too exclusively connected, but which is deeply involved in it. Its central principle is the simple fact that Christ, by His personal act, and by the shedding of His blood, has made reconciliation between us and God. In St. John's comprehensive expression, 'He Himself is the propitiation for our sins.' He, in His love, and in His life and death, appeals alike to the love of God and to the heart of man. It is the personal Saviour, in His personal sacrifice, who constitutes this propitiation. Or consider again the truth of His Divinity. Its supreme practical importance is sufficiently discerned from the fact that it is the necessary condition of our belief in the simple assurance of the text in all its fulness. For it is because our Lord is God, as well as man, that He is able to be everywhere present to every soul, at all times, that we can believe that He is ever with us, perpetually speaking by His Spirit to our hearts. None but one who is God as well as man can be a Saviour in that comprehensive sense in which our Lord constantly proclaims Himself, and in which it is our blessing to believe on Him. None else can be with us through life and death; to none other can we commend our souls at our last hours. The loftiest heights of Christian truth are thus involved in this text, when given its ample meaning.

Not less involved in it are the heights and depths of all human experience, if they are to issue in blessing and not in despair. The hour will come to all of us when our flesh and heart will fail us, when the eye will be dim and the mind be unable to retain any but the simplest thought; but in that hour to the Christian, the one word Saviour, the name of Jesus, will suffice to assure us that the eternal God is with us, and that underneath us are the everlasting arms. And as this short and simple Gospel is the one adequate comfort in death, not less in life does it transform our whole moral position. Its effect is to render possible moral aims and moral efforts, which would otherwise be impracticable and desperate. Consider a man as standing alone amidst his fellows, and left to no other influence than theirs, and it cannot but be recognized that there are limits to the possibilities of his moral achievements. On natural grounds, he cannot rise above himself and the influences with which he is surrounded. There are consequences of his past sins which he cannot shake off, and it might even seem harsh to ask too much of him. But once recognize that there is a Divine Saviour at his side, and all is changed. No aim is then too lofty, and no hope too bold. It is not too much, then, to address to him even the command, 'Be ye perfect, even as your Father which is in heaven is perfect.' The Sermon on the Mount, in which that expression occurs, affords a most striking illustration of this truth. Had it been addressed to men in their natural condition, there would be something terrible in its unsparing severity, in the relentlessness with which it exposes the fatal vice of even passing thoughts and looks and words, and in the narrowness and straitness of the path which it marks out. But it is not addressed to men in their natural condition. It is addressed by a Saviour to those whom He is ready to save, and it is clenched, and enforced, and rendered tolerable to our weakness by that Saviour's evangelical promise, 'Ask, and it shall be given you. . . . If ye, being evil, know how to give good gifts unto your children, how much more shall your Father which is in heaven give good things to them that ask Him?' With a Saviour at our side, but only under this condition, that Sermon is the revelation of an ideal at which every soul may aim, and which every soul may hope some day to attain. We are capable, with that aid, of ever-increasing growth in truth, in righteousness, and in all grace, and of ultimate union with truth, and righteousness, and glory itself. This blessing is ours because of the truth declared in the text—because there is a Saviour, who will save His people from their sins. Such is the profound significance of the angelic announcement which is recorded at the outset of the Gospels. It is the key to all that follows; and only in proportion as we apprehend the depth of its meaning and its supreme importance, can we be in a position to appreciate either the historic facts or the spiritual verities which are involved in the life and ministry of our Lord.

Let me remark, in conclusion, that the truth of this announcement has been tested by a long and blessed experience. Above all, in a degree which has too rarely since been approached, was it experienced and verified by the early Church. In the strength which this promise of a Saviour afforded them, and with the grace which that Saviour gave them, they sprang forward with irrepressible eagerness in the pursuit of all Christian graces. The new world of the fruits of the Spirit, love, joy, peace, gentleness, goodness, faith, meekness, temperance —faith, hope, and charity—seemed to open itself to their hopes and energies, and they lived and breathed as new creatures in Christ. No delight seemed to them comparable to that of this spiritual career, and every moment seemed lost which did not advance them in likeness to their Saviour. That blessing and that glorious career are open to all of us. No soul need be so saddened by failure, or so oppressed by weakness, or so burdened by sorrow and pain, as to forego it. The message of the text is adequate to renew the spiritual life of every soul who is privileged to receive it. We may well feel, as we contemplate our past, our present, or our future, that we cannot save ourselves. But our Christian faith is summed up in the acknowledgment of One who was called Jesus, because He shall save His people from their sins. Let us only be among His people; let us trust Him, obey Him, pray to Him, work with Him; and we are assured by His promise, and by the unvarying experience of Christians, that He will guide, support, and deliver us.

LECTURE V

THE MIRACLES OF OUR LORD

"And when Jesus was entered into Capernaum, there came unto Him a centurion, beseeching Him, and saying, Lord, my servant lieth at home sick of the palsy, grievously tormented. And Jesus saith unto him, I will come and heal him. The centurion answered and said, Lord, I am not worthy that thou shouldest come under my roof: but speak the word only, and my servant shall be healed. For I am a man under authority, having soldiers under me: and I say to this man, Go, and he goeth; and to another, Come, and he cometh; and to my servant, Do this, and he doeth it. When Jesus heard it, He marvelled, and said to them that followed, Verily I say unto you, I have not found so great faith, no, not in Israel."—*St. Matt.* viii. 5-10.

THE eighth chapter of St. Matthew is a portion of that Gospel which has peculiar value from the light which it throws upon our Lord's miracles. The eighth and ninth chapters contain a record of ten of His miracles, and these are one half of the whole number recorded by that evangelist; while it is also to be noticed that this record of all these works of supernatural power and mercy immediately follows the Sermon on the Mount. It may first be observed that this close juxtaposition of two such portions of the narrative is but one of many instances of the impossibility of separating the testimony of the evangelists to the miraculous works of our Lord from their testimony to His moral teaching. Their credibility in reporting the latter is fully admitted by many persons who hesitate to admit it with respect to the former. But their admitted faithfulness in the one portion of their narratives cannot but add immense weight to their testimony in the other. In the three chapters preceding this miraculous record, St. Matthew has preserved to us, with a vividness and force of which the most sceptical are sensible, a long discourse by our Lord of supreme import, which is universally felt to embody some of His most characteristic teaching. Men of very diverse views, even among those who are most hostile to our faith as a whole, feel in their inmost consciences that these were the words of one who spoke to men with an authority beyond that of any other teacher, and accept them as a true account of the greatest moral instruction ever heard. Now, is it not a strange paradox, to suppose that a writer who was sufficiently imbued with the spirit of the teaching of the Sermon on the Mount to record its substance with a force and accuracy which have penetrated to the hearts of all subsequent generations, should immediately, and, as it were, almost in the same breath, pass to a similarly long narrative of purely illusive reminiscences? In the one passage, we are surrounded with a blaze of moral and spiritual light, piercing to the very thoughts and intents of the heart, burning up all falsehood in word or deed, all hypocrisy and unreality; and in the next passage some would ask us to believe that we find ourselves in an atmosphere of illusion, credulity, and uncertainty! Such a transition from absolute light—light undimmed, unobscured by a single shadow, unperverted by a single false colour, is certainly unknown elsewhere, and may well be regarded as inconceivable. But it is the same throughout the Gospels. Many of our Lord's most precious sayings are inseparably bound up with His miracles, arise out of them and point their lessons. The two are indissolubly united; and the Sermon on the Mount is thus itself the best guarantee for the miraculous narratives which immediately follow it.

But there is a special characteristic about these two chapters which adds further weight to this consideration. The record of these miracles appears to be placed in this particular connection by express design; for they are narrated with a marked deviation from chronological order. There appears no question, from the narratives of the other evangelists, that the miracles here narrated did not all follow immediately—even if any of them did—the delivery of the Sermon on the Mount. St. Matthew would seem to have grouped them together here, with little reference to the order in which they occurred, for a special purpose; and it is natural to suppose that this purpose was to illustrate one particular aspect of our Lord's ministry. He had just given a long and comprehensive example of our Lord's teaching, and he immediately proceeds to exhibit a similarly comprehensive illustration of His working. Such, at least, is the effect produced; and considering that the various incidents in these two chapters are, as has been said, brought together out of their order, we may well suppose that such was the design. In fact, in the twenty-third verse of the fourth chapter, St. Matthew has summarized our Lord's ministry under these two heads of teaching and healing. 'Jesus,' we read, 'went about all Galilee, teaching in their synagogues, and preaching the gospel of the kingdom, and healing all manner of sickness and all manner of disease among the people.' Of this teaching St. Matthew proceeds to give us an account in the Sermon on the Mount; and of these works of healing he next gives an account in the eighth and ninth chapters. At the end of the ninth chapter, in the thirty-fifth verse, this ministry, in its two-fold character, is again summed up in almost the same words. 'Jesus went about all the cities and villages, teaching in their synagogues, and preaching the gospel of the kingdom, and healing every sickness and every disease among the people.' Then the evangelist passes to describe the extension of the same ministerial work by the mission of the twelve apostles, and afterwards proceeds to other topics, such as that contest with the Scribes and Pharisees which ended in our Saviour's death. There thus appears a very clear and instructive order in the arrangement of the Gospel; and the evangelist would seem most carefully to impress upon us what were the two main elements in our Saviour's ministerial work, and their intimate connection with each other. He was at once a Teacher and a Saviour; in the one character summoning men to repent, because the kingdom of heaven was at hand—a kingdom with severer laws, sterner demands, more exalted ideals, than any that had been heard of in this world; but, on the other hand, revealing Himself as the royal possessor of new and glorious powers, and able to save all who trusted Him from the evils, whether bodily or spiritual, under which they were suffering, and of which His teaching revealed the terrible danger and misery.

It cannot but be felt that this second manifestation is at once a most gracious and a most necessary addition to the former. Our Lord had just been exhibiting a picture of the perfection of human life, spiritually, morally, and even physically. He had described, in the Sermon on the Mount, a character of perfect righteousness, gentleness, purity, truth, mercy, and faith. Take St. Paul's summary of Christian virtues, and you will find it an abridgment of the Sermon on the Mount: 'The fruit of the Spirit is love, joy, peace, long-suffering, gentleness, goodness, faith, meekness, temperance.' These graces are enlarged upon by our Lord, and exhibited in contrast to the imperfections presented by men's actual characters and conduct. But He does not confine His description to the spiritual or moral life. He assures His disciples that in proportion as they lived in this spirit of faith, seeking first the kingdom of God and His righteousness, all other things should be added unto them. 'Consider the lilies of the field,' He says, 'how they grow; they toil not, neither do they spin: and yet I say unto you that even Solomon in all his glory was not arrayed like one of these. Wherefore, if God so clothe the grass of the field, which to-day is, and to-morrow is cast unto the oven, shall He not much more clothe you, O ye of little faith?' It was this combination of complete soundness or salvation in body and soul, to which the prophets of His people had looked forward, uniting in one glorious vision all spiritual, moral, and physical perfection. The passage which St. Luke tells us He Himself chose from the prophet Isaiah, vividly depicts such a revelation— 'The Spirit of the Lord is upon me, because

He hath anointed me to preach the Gospel to the poor; He hath sent me to heal the broken-hearted, to preach deliverance to the captives, and recovery of sight to the blind, to set at liberty them that are bruised, to preach the acceptable year of the Lord. 'This day,' He said, 'is this Scripture fulfilled in your ears.' But how could it have been fulfilled, unless, in addition to proclaiming anew these promises, in addition to enlightening the consciences and stimulating the moral energies of His people, He had actually exerted that healing and saving power of which He spoke?

Would it not, in fact, have seemed, we may almost say, a cruel mockery of human hopes and aspirations, had our Lord been unable to do more than hold up before men more perfect ideals than any they had ever dreamed of, without stretching out His hand of power to enable them to realize such visions? There has been no sadder experience, throughout the history of mankind, than the desperate, if not despairing, efforts of noble spirits to hold up such ideals before themselves and their fellows, and the disappointment caused by the ever-repeated failure to attain them. The spectacle or the experience has, in age after age, turned some passionate souls to cynicism, and has tempted the mass of men to acquiescence in low standards, as all they could attain to. But endeavour for a moment to realize what a terrible exhibition of this weakness would have been afforded, if the words of the Gospels had presented to us nothing but the Saviour's exhortations to perfection, and no instances of His power to ensure their fulfilment. We should have contemplated, as it were, a glorious and inaccessible height, sensible above all things that it was for ever beyond the reach of ourselves and of our fellows. But at this point the miracles of the Gospels come in, to give, as it were, a reality to all these visions, hopes, and aspirations. We see all the evils and miseries which afflict mankind driven away at the Saviour's word, in response to the prayer of earnest faith. A leper comes and worships Him, saying, 'Lord, if thou wilt, thou canst make me clean.' And Jesus puts forth His hand and touches him, saying, 'I will, be thou clean;' and immediately his leprosy is cleansed. They bring unto Him many that are possessed with devils, and He casts out the spirits with His word, and heals all that are sick. He speaks the word only, and the centurion's servant is healed. There arises a great tempest in the sea, and His disciples come to Him, saying, 'Lord, save us;' and He arises and rebukes the winds and the sea, and there is a great calm. The publicans and sinners, the morally sick, come and sit down with Him, and He receives them as their physician, summons one of them from the receipt of custom, and transforms him into an Apostle and Evangelist. He heals the blind, and raises the dead, until the multitudes exclaim, 'It was never so seen in Israel.' This is the one harmonious and glorious picture which is presented by our Lord in His combined work of teaching and healing. To arouse in us a longing for all perfection, and by His supernatural might to bestow it upon all faithful hearts, these are His two-fold offices, equally characteristic of Him, equally necessary for us.

We have, in these days more particularly, to beware of allowing this complete image of our Lord to be marred by any tendency to throw His miraculous works in the back-ground, or to draw any veil over them. Our chief privilege, in our weakness, ignorance, and corruption, is to believe that we have this Almighty Saviour ever at our side, and that we can trust Him to protect us, to cleanse us, to deliver us from evil, as really as those among whom He lived when upon earth. The preciousness of these narratives to ourselves depends upon their being an exhibition of the relation in which we ourselves stand to the Lord Jesus Christ, and in which He stands to us. When we recite the creed, we are not, as is sometimes insinuated, asserting mere abstract dogmas respecting the nature of the Godhead, but are renewing and refreshing the blessed belief that the Lord Jesus, who is here described to us as preaching the Gospel of the Kingdom, and healing every sickness and every disease among the people, is the same yesterday, to-day, and for ever; that, as God, He is ever with us; that He sits at the right hand of the Father, commanding, for our sakes, all power in heaven and earth, and by His Spirit ever working among us, to deliver us from our sins and evils.

But we know too well the objections which are raised against such a belief. Where, it is asked, are the evidences of the Saviour's interpositions in the affairs of ordinary life, in the natural course of physical existence? Miraculous signs, such as those recorded in the Gospels, are no longer exhibited among us, and how are we to believe in a constant personal action which is not open to our perception? Now, the first and most direct reply to such objections was anticipated by the Centurion, whose signal display of faith is recorded in the text as having aroused our Lord's admiration. He realized, from his experience of the methods of action in human affairs, that there was no occasion, for the purpose of our Lord's intervention, of any extraordinary and conspicuous manifestation. If he, a man under authority, yet had soldiers under him, and could say to this man, Go, and he goeth; and to another, Come, and he cometh; and to his servant,

Do this, and he doeth it; our Lord had but to speak the word to those natural elements of which He was the creator and master, and His will would be surely, though it might be silently, executed.

But the excellence of the Centurion's faith in this respect deserves a more particular consideration, and it will be more apparent by contrast with two opposite states of mind. The contrast to it which our Lord chiefly encountered was the peculiar disposition of the Jews, who, except they saw signs and wonders, would not believe. They fully recognized the existence of a Divine Power possessing command over all the forces of nature; but they would not believe in our Lord's ability to exert it, or in His readiness to aid them, unless it were manifested by some signal and extraordinary means. But there is another state of mind, akin to this in reality, and yet contrasted with it, which is prevalent at the present day. The form of unbelief which we have to encounter—and to encounter in ourselves, no doubt, as well as in others—is not one which craves for startling and overpowering instances of divine interposition, but one which doubts the reality of personal interposition at all, on the part of God, in the course of nature and in human life. To the Jews that interposition had, so to say, become so common and familiar an idea that they thought nothing of it, and scarcely regarded it as specially concerning them, unless it were exhibited in some exceptional form. To many among ourselves, on the other hand, the idea has become so unfamiliar that we find a difficulty in applying it to every-day life; and because we see no signs and wonders, we, too, do not believe. Starting in the opposite direction, we have come round to the same point as the Jews. Modern thought is absorbed and fascinated by the contemplation of the order of nature and the constancy of its methods. Fixing its attention, almost exclusively, on the impersonal part of nature, it fails to penetrate to the personality behind; and thus—even, it is to be feared, to many true Christian hearts—the intense conviction expressed in the Psalms of the living God being present with us, and directly acting upon us in every moment of our existence, controlling for us every circumstance of our lives, and ordering all that concerns ourselves and others, and the course of the world at large, in accordance with His will, with His approval and disapproval, and with His own spiritual purposes—this realization of the personal presence and action of the living God—in many cases, alas! absolutely denied and excluded—is, it is to be feared, in many others grievously enfeebled.

Now, that which forms the great and abiding wonder of the faith of the Centurion is that, by one simple observation, he supplies the conclusive and permanent answer to all these doubts and denials. As Luther puts it, with his usual vividness, 'This heathen soldier turns theologian, and begins to dispute in as fine and Christian-like a manner as would suffice for a man who had been many years Doctor of Divinity.' He cuts the knot at once, by that bold reasoning by analogy from man to God, of which our Lord's teaching is so full, and which is involved in the cardinal doctrines of the Gospel, such as the Divine Fatherhood and the forgiveness of sins. He says, simply, that the kind of action which men exhibit must be possible for God. It is impossible for Him to be more restricted in His action than His creatures; and if they are able, by subordinate agencies, to carry out their will, and to modify, by the interposition of that will, what would otherwise be the natural course of events, it is inconceivable that it should be impossible for Him to do the same.

The force of this argument should be vastly enhanced to us by that development of science and civilization which has been produced since the Centurion's time, and which is sometimes ungratefully used to obscure its truth. Let us realize how, in the present day, a single human will, at the centre of a great nation, or, rather, of a great empire like this, can make itself obeyed to the very extremities of the world, by means of a subtle electrical current, scarcely perceptible to the touch, and during a great part of its course buried in obscurity under vast oceans; and with what reason can it be denied that the Creator of all these subtle forces, in whose hands they all lie, can silently modify, by an act of His will, the course of any event in His universe, and that He can say to His servants, as we to ours, Do this, and it is done? When we, with our utterly imperfect knowledge, can so modify the action of natural forces as to neutralize a disease by a little counter poison, or revivify the nervous forces of life by galvanic currents, must it not seem the height of all unreason to deny an infinitely superior, and at the same time, infinitely more mysterious and invisible capacity, to Him who created at once these forces, and the human brain which makes use of them? The simple principle, in a word, to which the Centurion appeals may be stated in our more scientific way, by saying that whatever forces there are in nature, must reside within the maker of nature, only in an infinitely enhanced degree; and the point on which it is more especially necessary to insist in applying this principle, is that which the Centurion grasped—namely, that the powers of man, of man's intellect and will, must, above all things, be regarded as an example of one form of the divine action. The kind of things which man can do, God can certainly do; and if modern men of science can modify the operation of nature by methods which, to men not so scientific, would be incomprehensible, and even invisible, certainly God can modify nature and control it by means which, even to men of science, are similarly incomprehensible and invisible.

There seems, in fact, to lurk an extraordinary sophism in the offence which is taken at so-called anthropomorphism. Men observe the operation of the inanimate forces of nature, and deduce from them the methods of God's operation. There, they will say, you observe the course of His action; and you notice its absolute regularity, and the absence of any indication that we can detect of its disturbance by personal action and will. But the moment the moralist, or the theologian, points to another sphere of nature—that of human nature, which is nature still—and argues from it in a similar manner, regarding it as a revelation of part, at all events, of God's method of action, we are denounced as anthropomorphic. Be it so. But what is the scientific conception but—if I may be allowed to coin the word—physico-morphism? They see the likeness and reflection of God in nature; we see the image and reflection of God in man; and why not the one as well as the other? The corruption of our moral nature creates, indeed, a gulf between us and Him. But considered from the point of view of a physical philosopher, man is not only a part of nature, but the highest and most completely developed part. By all means let us learn all that natural philosophers can tell us of the Divine nature, and methods, and power, from the inanimate and irrational creation; but let them not refuse to take into account what we can tell them, or rather what their own hearts can tell them, respecting God's nature, His power and the method of His action, as exhibited in the mind and will of man. You discern in nature an order which, in some sense, is immutable; and if you admit a Divine mind at all, you attribute a similar order, and a similar immutability, to that mind. Then let us argue in the same way from our own nature; and if we see the very noblest expressions of human nature in our love, our hatred, our wrath, our mercy, our repentance, our forgiveness, let us acknowledge, on the same principle, that these also are a reflex, however faint, of Divine perfections, and let us not shrink from recognizing, in the language of the Scriptures, that the Creator of those emotions loves and hates, and is wrathful and merciful, and repents and forgives. And if we hold in our hands a vast complexity of agencies, human, animal, physical, chemical, which come as we bid them come, and go as we bid them go, in accordance, not with any immutable order of external nature, but in obedience to our intellectual designs and moral intentions, to fulfil our love or our enmity, our justice or our mercy, with what reason can we doubt that He too—but with a completeness, an invisibleness, a continuousness, a supremacy, of which we have no conception—is controlling every physical element, and every circumstance which surrounds us? Argue from nature exclusive of man, and you may acquiesce in the hard mechanical views which alone it suggests to you. Argue from nature with man, and man's actions, and man's will, included within it, and you will agree with Luther that the Centurion was a great Doctor of Divinity.

In short, any objections against the daily moral interposition of a Divine will in the course of nature, on the ground of the immutability of physical laws and of their action, is equally, as is now candidly confessed, an argument against the independent personal action of a human will. Man's body, in all its functions, is a part of the whole sum of nature. It enters the sphere in which all the laws of physical nature work. It is subject to the law of the conservation of force, and to every other physical consideration by which personal divine will is supposed to be excluded. And yet, in spite of this, and side by side with it, we are all acting on each other by moral forces; our physical actions are prompted by moral motives, by intellectual designs, by determinations of will. But this, it is sometimes replied, is an illusion. You seem to have a free will; but you have not; you are a link in the chain of causation, and your apparent morality is a physical product. For the purposes of such an argument as the present, this is a mere dispute about words. Let your will, your love, your intellect, be what you please. All the theologian is concerned to maintain is that the Divine will, the Divine love, the Divine wisdom, can act and does act, in a similar manner; and that if we say to one subordinate agent, from moral motives, and for moral purposes, Go, and it goeth, and to another, Come, and it cometh, and to our servants, Do this, and they do it, our Creator, the source and eternal strength of all these powers, is perpetually employing in a similar manner, and for similar motives—albeit with an exaltation of their character far beyond our conceptions—the innumerable agencies which are under His command.

It follows from considerations such as these that it is not necessary for us to see conspicuous instances of supernatural operations around us, in order to be assured that, in the words of our office for the visitation of the sick, 'Almighty God is the Lord of life and death, and of all things to them pertaining, as youth, strength, health, age, weakness, and sickness;' so that whatever may befall us, the one thing we may 'know certainly' is, that 'it is God's visitation.' But still, some one may repeat, we do not see it; we discern no traces of this personal action by the unseen God. And because we do not see it—we, with our limited perceptions; we, who are conscious that we are but on the threshold of the mysteries of nature; we, who cannot so much as foresee a snow-storm the day before it arrives—are we to conclude from this incapacity of vision to a limitation of the action of Him, 'who giveth snow like wool, who scattereth the hoar frost like ashes; who casteth forth His ice like morsels; who can stand before His cold? who sendeth out His word and melteth them? who causeth His wind to blow and the waters flow?' We may, as a rule, not see it. That divine interposition is mysterious, and often impenetrable. But this, at least, must be said on this point—there are some things apparent to those who have eyes to see and hearts to understand, which will not force themselves upon the attention of those who are indifferent to them, or prejudiced against them; and in this matter, similarly, the faithful Christian has eyes to see things which are often obscure to those who are destitute of his faith; and they are none the less realities because others cannot perceive them. To many a faithful and thoughtful heart the experience of life is a strong confirmation of the assurance that the Saviour has been at its side, shielding it in many a critical moment of life from the dangers with which it was threatened, ensuring that it should not be tempted above that which it was able to bear, and with every temptation making a way of escape. In many moments of serious and humble reflection on the past, the reality of such interpositions will come home to the soul. We recognize—we feel forced with profound gratitude to recognize—glimpses of the Divine hand, shielding us by a touch, which was at the time imperceptible, from some terrible moral or physical calamity. Reverent and faithful souls, who walk through the world with the consciousness that the Saviour is at their side, are often vouchsafed, as the Scriptures and the records of the Church bear witness, such apprehensions of His presence, and learn more and more to look up to Him with the trust of experience, as well as of faith. Such experiences may not be arguments for convincing unbelievers, though they are certainly facts which have a claim to be taken into account. But they are, at least, strong encouragements and assurances to the faithful; and perhaps we ought to ask ourselves whether, especially in times like the present, we are not called upon to divest ourselves, more frequently than we are wont, of the reserve—or is it the timidity—which clings to us, and to join more openly, and more boldly, in the language of the Psalmist, —' O bless our God, ye people, and make the voice of His praise to be heard ; which holdeth our soul in life, and suffereth not our feet to be moved. . . . Come and hear, all ye that fear God, and I will declare what He hath done for my soul. Verily, God hath heard me; He hath attended to the voice of my prayer. Blessed be God, who hath not turned away my prayer, nor His mercy from me.'

But there remains another observation, more open to ordinary criticism, with which it is important to conclude any consideration of this subject, and which is naturally suggested by a review of this portion of St. Matthew's Gospel. This is, that we observe clear indications, alike in the Sermon on the Mount, and in the records of the miracles themselves, that the natural order of the Saviour's working is not so much directly upon the bodies of men and their physical circumstances, as upon their spirits, and that His physical miracles were designed to lead their thoughts to His spiritual power, and thus to ensure the regeneration of their lower nature by means of their higher. Our Lord expressly points to this use of His miracles in the case of His cure of the sick of the palsy, which is recorded in the midst of this collection of His works of power, at the commencement of St. Matthew's ninth chapter. 'He said unto the sick of the palsy, Son, be of good cheer; thy sins be forgiven thee;' and when 'certain of the Scribes said within themselves, This man blasphemeth,' Jesus, 'knowing their thoughts, said, Wherefore think ye evil in your hearts? For whether is easier; to say, Thy sins be forgiven thee; or to say, Arise and walk? But that ye may know that the Son of Man hath power on earth to forgive sins, (then saith He to the sick of the palsy,) Arise, take up thy bed, and go unto thine house.' The ultimate purpose of that miracle, therefore, was to lead those before whom it was wrought to look to the same gracious hand for the invisible, but still supernatural, grace of spiritual forgiveness and moral regeneration. He who could command a physical miracle, and prove His power by instantly effecting it, might be appealed to with confidence for the still higher miracles of the spiritual sphere.

But in thus pointing men above the physical to the spiritual, our Lord, as has just been observed, is acting in full harmony with His teaching in the Sermon on the Mount. It is through righteousness that He teaches His disciples to seek for the blessings of this life. 'Take,' He says, 'no thought, saying, What shall we eat? or, What shall we drink? or, Wherewithal shall we be clothed? (For after all these things do the Gentiles seek:) for your heavenly Father knoweth that ye have need of all these things. But seek ye first the kingdom of God, and His righteousness; and all these things shall be added unto you.' This exhortation may be applied with eminent instruction to the subsequent exercise of our Lord's saving power, first in His ministry, and afterwards in the history of His Church. His miracles, here recorded, were wrought during the darkest hours of human nature, at the time of its deepest despair, to awaken men's faith, and to lead them to trust Him for deliverance. But it was in strict conformity with the constitution of their nature, and with His highest designs for their good, that this saving work should for the most part be directed to their spiritual deliverance; and that He should, as it were, lead them to work out their physical salvation by means of their moral. It is by moral evil that physical evil has been brought upon us; and could we be delivered from moral evil, we should be saved from physical.

It is contrary, in fact, to all the analogy of God's dealings, in nature and in grace alike, to excuse us from the due exercise, to the utmost of our powers, of our natural faculties. During His stay on earth, He took us, as it were, by the hand, and placed us in the right path, and He has since been training us in all the ways of spiritual, moral, intellectual, and physical truth. Undoubtedly the physical condition of mankind has been vastly ameliorated, and is being daily more and more ameliorated, by the elevation of their moral nature through the Gospel, and through spiritual grace; and we may well believe that infinite possibilities in this respect still remain, which God designs us to realize in the exercise, under that spiritual influence, of our natural powers. He would have us exert ourselves in all ways to the utmost, according to His own lesson in one of His miracles, 'Gathering up the fragments that nothing be lost.' But what a supreme blessing to be assured that He is ever with us, to bless and to complete every effort that we can make! The law laid down by the Apostle applies to our whole career. God will not protect us from all temptation, nor deliver us at one stroke from the evils which we have brought upon ourselves. But He is ever near, as with the disciples in the storm, to ensure that we shall not be overwhelmed; He 'is faithful, and will not suffer us to be tempted above that we are able, but will with the temptation also make a way to escape, that we may be able to bear it.' Under His guidance, and with His aid, a way of deliverance from all evils is ever open to us. If we have failed to realize it, let us ask ourselves how far we have appealed to Him with the faith which is exhibited in those examples of His saving power which St. Matthew here brings before us. The rule of His working has ever been,

'As thou hast believed, so be it done unto thee.' All things—all things necessary for our spiritual health, and for our physical welfare also, so far as the latter is compatible with the former—are still, as ever, possible to him that believeth; and let us pray, at the conclusion of such meditations, 'Lord, I believe, help thou mine unbelief.'

LECTURE VI

THE PASSION AND DEATH OF OUR LORD

"Whom God hath set forth to be a propitiation through faith in His blood, to declare His righteousness for the remission of sins that are past, through the forbearance of God; to declare, I say, at this time His righteousness: that He might be just, and the justifier of him which believeth in Jesus."—*Rom.* iii. 25, 26.

THE history of our Saviour's Passion is a subject which must be approached at any time with feelings of deep apprehension; and we must above all things feel reluctant to bring its sacred and solemn associations into connexion with discussions which have anything of a controversial nature. At the same time it would be impracticable to form a just view of the general character of the Gospel narratives without considering that history, were it only in consequence of the large space in them which it occupies. On an average, the narrative of the Passion occupies not less than one-tenth of the four Gospels, while of the rest of St. John's Gospel, a great portion may be said to lead up to it. The character, therefore, of the evangelical narratives on this subject must go very far to determine their general credibility, and must afford no inadequate measure of the power with which they have apprehended and presented to us the essential elements of our Lord's life and work.

Now it is very remarkable, from this point of view, that there is practically no difference of opinion as to the credibility, in all substantial points, of this momentous portion of the story of the Gospels. Thus Dr. Hase, already referred to as one of the most distinguished and venerable of the theologians of Germany, and sufficiently rationalistic to hold very sceptical conclusions as to our Lord's Resurrection and Ascension, says that in respect of this period of our Lord's life, all four Gospels go side by side with each other, and exhibit in their variations only the various sides and conceptions of the same occurrence; and that up to the hour of our Lord's death, all is narrated with the particularity with which men are wont to preserve the memory of the last moments of a beloved and great man.* This result is the more remarkable because there are some real difficulties in point of chronological harmony in this part of the narrative, as, for instance, with respect to the evening on which the Lord's Supper was instituted. But it is

---

* *Geschichte Jesu*, § 92, p. 525; Leipzig, 1876.

felt that the narrative in each Gospel bears the most unmistakeable marks of truth, and that no such difficulties of detail, which are probably only due to our own ignorance of some reconciling facts, can affect their authority.

In fact, by a sort of unconscious agreement, however men may dispute the truth of other parts of the Gospels, they tacitly assume the truth of the story of the Passion; and among unbelievers, no less than believers, Jesus Christ is regarded as having suffered the martyrdom which the evangelists describe, and as having suffered it for the reasons which they allege. It would seem there is something in the intense reality of the narrative which compels belief, and makes men feel instinctively that the narrators are telling the simple and terrible truth. The perfect simplicity of the narration, and yet its revelation of depths of sorrow and suffering, and at the same time of the loftiest truth and majesty, in our Lord—all this is felt, and is practically confessed, to be beyond the power of any invention. The absence of a single false note, of a word or a comment, inconsistent with the awful character of the scene, compels men to acknowledge that they are in the presence of absolute realities.

There is one other mark of complete sincerity and truthfulness in the narration which deserves particular attention, and which has been forcibly dwelt upon by the eminent French preacher, M. Bersier, in his great sermon on the testimony of the Apostles.* These narratives, as we have seen, are written by Apostles, or by friends of Apostles, and the writers do not shrink from describing their own conduct, or that of their masters, as of a character which nothing but an absolute submission to truth could have induced them to confess. They frankly acknowledge, as M. Bersier observes, that at the supreme hour of their Master's fate, they trembled like children and cowards. 'They confess that when their Master, who had never ceased to love them, and to bless them with a divine tenderness, had been betrayed by one of themselves, and led before His judges, they all forsook him and fled; and that the very one of them who had sworn to remain faithful to Him, denied Him three times at the challenge of a servant-maid. Without taking any notice of the scandal and disgrace of such a story, they relate it in full detail, without omitting a word. They were about to proclaim to the world the cross of Jesus Christ, and to point men to it as the means of salvation; and yet they dare to acknowledge that, at the hour when that cross was erected, they deserted it like cowards, leaving to weak women the honour of attending their

---

* *Sermons*, par E. Bersier; Tome vi., *Le Témoignage des Apôtres*, pp. 50–53.

Master in His agony, leaving to a robber the honour of being the first to announce the eternal royalty of the Crucified, just as three days afterwards Mary Magdalen was allowed the honour of being the first to proclaim the triumph of the risen Christ.' If there is something amazing in the rigid truthfulness which confessed all these lamentable facts, it establishes for the narrators a claim for the most ample trust when recording events of a more welcome character.

Indeed, apart from the evidence of sincerity afforded by these confessions of the Apostles respecting themselves, it is sufficiently remarkable that they should have preserved with such fulness the story of their Master's humiliation. Christ crucified was, we are told by St. Paul, ' unto the Jews a stumbling-block, and unto the Greeks foolishness.' It was a constant reproach to Christians that they worshipped a man who had been crucified as a malefactor. The main fact, of course, could not be disguised. But that the evangelical writers should have so diligently preserved what might otherwise have been forgotten—all the minute circumstances of their Master's humiliation, the very weakness of His flesh, and His shrinking, in the garden, from the cup He had to drink, all those marks, in fact, of His human weakness which were obliterated by His resurrection—this is an instance of truthfulness which seems at least incompatible with any legendary origin of the narratives, at a time when our Lord was contemplated in the glory of His ascension, and of His session at the right hand of God. But whatever impression of truthfulness, and of intense reality in detail, is thus created by the history of the Passion, must in justice be allowed to reflect back over the whole preceding history. To accept, as many persons seem unconsciously to do, the story of Christ's Passion, forming so considerable and important a part of the whole Gospel, as profoundly true, and yet to deal with the remainder as open to the most unsparing suspicion, is not, it would seem, a proceeding that can be reasonably justified. The story of our Lord's death has established a claim to be accepted as a truthful record of the most solemn event in the world's history; and the four witnesses by whom that story is told, and who are fully agreed together respecting it, have for that reason a claim to be regarded as at least among the most trustworthy witnesses to any other historical facts they may relate.

We may be spared, therefore, for our present purpose, the ungracious task of critical discussions on this topic, and may address ourselves to more vital considerations. It has been the purpose of these Lectures, not merely to vindicate the historic credibility of the Gospel narratives, but to illustrate the spiritual and moral significance of the leading facts which they record; and in no part of our subject are such considerations so urgently incumbent upon us. As is indicated by the space which the narrative holds in the Gospels, the whole mystery of our Lord's life and work centres around His Passion. To this, in fact, the history in the Gospels points from their commencement. Our Lord's forerunner pointed to Him at the outset as 'The Lamb of God which taketh away the sin of the world,' that is to say, the sacrificial victim who should suffer for that sin, and by whose death it should be done away. Similarly, He Himself, at the commencement of His ministry, in His interview with Nicodemus, proclaimed this as the essential part of His mission. 'As Moses lifted up the serpent in the wilderness, even so must the Son of Man be lifted up: that whosoever believeth in Him should not perish, but have everlasting life.' At a later date, in the transfiguration, when He was for a moment revealed to His disciples in glory, the two great prophets who appeared communing with Him 'spake of His decease which He should accomplish at Jerusalem.' The whole of His ministry, in a word, led up to that death, and was consummated in it. Accordingly, St. Paul's account of His message to the Corinthians is an exact summary of the most important part of the Gospel narrative—

'I delivered unto you first of all that which I also received, how that Christ died for our sins according to the Scriptures; and that He was buried, and that He rose again the third day according to the Scriptures.' The Creed, in passing so swiftly from His birth to His death, is thus in complete harmony with His own teaching respecting His ministerial work.

This consideration has a decisive bearing upon the attempts which have been frequently made, especially of late years, to exhibit our Lord solely as a preacher of righteousness, alike by word and by example, and to represent as alien from His teaching the prominence which is given in the Epistles, particularly in those of St. Paul, to the doctrine, or rather to the fact, of the Atonement. But there is one circumstance singularly independent of any critical debates, and resting on the plainest historical evidence, which is more than sufficient to refute such misconceptions. That circumstance is the institution of the Lord's Supper. Alike from the Evangelists and from St. Paul, we learn that our Lord Jesus Christ, in the same night in which He was betrayed, instituted that sacrament in remembrance of Himself. It was to be, as it has been, the central memorial of the Saviour and of His work for us through all the ages of the Christian church. Instituted at that solemn moment, and for this supreme object, it cannot but be regarded as commemorating that peculiar aspect of our Lord's work which was paramount in its importance, and which it was above all things necessary that we should ever bear in mind. And what is this? Not His teaching, not His example, not His miracles, nay, not even His resurrection, but His death as a sacrifice for sin. In the account of the three Evangelists and of St. Paul of the words He used, there are the slight variations of form which frequently mark their reports, and which, in combination with their substantial agreement, afford such strong evidence of their independence and truthfulness. But this central conception is mentioned in all of them. St. Matthew and St. Mark, for instance, do not mention that when our Lord broke and distributed the bread He said that He was about to die for others; but they both tell us that when He took the cup He said, 'This is my blood of the New Testament, which is shed for many.' St. Paul, on the other hand, does not mention that when our Lord took the cup He said His blood was to be shed for others, but he tells us that when our Lord took the bread He said, 'This is my body, which is broken for you.' St. Luke combines the two accounts, by stating that our Lord declared His death to be a death for others, both when He broke the bread and when He gave the wine. 'He took bread and gave thanks, and brake it, and gave unto them, saying, This is my body, which is given for you; this do in remembrance of me. Likewise also the cup after supper, saying, This cup is the New Testament in my blood, which is shed for you.' There could not possibly have been a more solemn declaration on our Lord's part that the fact of His having died for our sins, and to procure their remission, was the one grand truth respecting Himself which He desired to be ever present and ever prominent in the thoughts of His people.

Now, in approaching this subject, we shall do best to endeavour, in the first place, to realize simply the historic significance of the fact of our Lord's Passion. The difficulties which have been felt of late years in apprehending the truth of the Atonement appear to be in great measure connected with a feeling that there is something arbitrary and artificial in the circumstances and conditions with which it is associated. Probably some partial expositions of the doctrine which, as a natural consequence of our imperfections, have been from time to time put forward as though they were a complete account of it, are in great measure responsible for these misapprehensions. It is no wonder, indeed, if in their efforts—efforts which they were bound to make—to apprehend the profoundest of all the truths respecting human nature and its relation to God, men have fallen short of the mighty reality, and have been induced to take refuge in systems to some extent of their own construction, and therefore more within their compass. There is, to say the least, great peril in all such attempts. But if, without presuming to attempt any theory on the subject, we concentrate our attention on the plain and terrible realities of the history, and on the revelation which its facts afford us of God and of Man, we may be able to lay hold of some of the great truths it exhibits, with at least sufficient clearness for the main purposes of our spiritual life.

Let us observe, then, in the first place, the momentous import of the history of the Passion, as exhibiting historically, and as a matter of fact, the condition of human nature at the time, and our Lord's relation to it. Those events cannot but be regarded, from almost any point of view, as affording the most fearful exhibition conceivable of the capacities of human nature for evil. I say from almost any point of view, because the main fact in the case is all but universally admitted. That fact is the perfection, the supreme truth, goodness, and beauty, of our Lord's life and teaching. Even those who do not regard Him as divine rarely admit any exception to His paramount claims in this respect. A few audacious critics have, perhaps, ventured to challenge some of His utterances as too enthusiastic for the practical necessities of life; but no such criticisms command any general attention. He now receives the general homage of the civilized world, as the ideal of moral and spiritual excellence. But nevertheless, and notwithstanding a beneficent public ministry of about three years, He was encountered with the most intense hatred, and was at length loaded with every kind of insult, and ignominiously and cruelly put to death. That human nature was capable of such conduct as this had, indeed, been foreseen by the profoundest philosopher of antiquity, in one of whose dialogues a comparison is drawn between the fate of the perfectly just, and of the perfectly unjust, man.* Plato there maintains that while the perfectly unjust man would enjoy every worldly honour, the just man 'will be scourged, racked, bound, have his eyes put out, and will at last be crucified.' There are few, however, who would have regarded such a terrible suggestion as more than a philosophical dream, unless it had been actually verified in experience; and now that it has been so verified, in the fearful realities of our Lord's Passion, it must ever remain the most amazing fact in the history of mankind. The simplest evidence that such a result is contrary to all natural antici-

---

* Plato's *Republic*, pp. 360-362. See Professor Jowett's translation, vol. ii. p. 18.

pations, is that we are perpetually judging of men and things by a rule which implies the contrary. Unconsciously, and by a kind of instinct, we attach great weight to the reputation which a man holds in common opinion, and in the judgment of his contemporaries; we hesitate to set ourselves against such a judgment, and are extremely reluctant to believe that large bodies of men can be united in detestation of truth, goodness, and beauty of character. Yet this, beyond all question, is what occurred in the case of our Lord.

The difficulty, it must be observed, cannot be escaped by throwing the whole blame upon the Jewish rulers, by whom the opposition to our Lord was organized. Their offence indeed was probably the deepest, with the exception of that of the false Apostle; for they were animated by motives of the most deliberate selfishness and calculating hypocrisy. This of itself would have seemed antecedently incredible. That a body of men who were occupied day by day, and hour by hour, with the most sacred functions and the holiest words, should all but unanimously conspire in a malignant and murderous plot against a person of perfect holiness and goodness—this is of itself astounding. But the Scribes and Pharisees were not alone. Though the common people had at other times heard our Lord gladly, they, too, deserted and repudiated Him at the last, and became the ready instruments of Pharisaic hatred. 'Then answered all the people, and said, His blood be on us, and on our children.' Nor is there any sign that this horrible impulse was repented of until the preaching of St. Peter, on the day of Pentecost, brought home to some of his hearers the enormity of the crime they had committed. Immediately after the crucifixion, we find the disciples meeting in secrecy, and apparently dreading a fate like that of their Master. Had it not been for the resurrection, the descent of the Holy Ghost and the preaching which followed it, there is nothing to show that any reaction against the crime would have arisen, even among the few thousands whose consciences St. Peter touched. The one absolutely perfect being who has ever appeared in the world would thus have been cast out of it ignominiously, by the practically unanimous consent of priests and religious leaders and rulers and people; and a mere handful of timid followers would alone have shown towards Him any real allegiance, and even that a wavering one. Among the evidences of our Lord's Divine prescience, none perhaps is so striking and conclusive as that in His parables, and in His private discourses with His disciples, these amazing results should have been calmly, systematically, and minutely predicted.

Now there can be no reason whatever for regarding the people who were guilty of this crime as in any way unworthy representatives of human nature in general. On the contrary, the Jews, in addition to their splendid natural endowments, had enjoyed a higher moral and spiritual training than any other people of that day. For centuries the Jewish teachers and people had had in their hands, as the food of their daily meditation, words which remain to this day the most powerful of all expositions of the essential principles of truth and righteousness. That which was possible for them is possible, and even probable, in the case of all men in like circumstances. The story of the Passion, therefore, must needs be regarded as casting its lurid and terrible light upon the condition and the dangers of all men by nature. The consideration is one, perhaps, which needs especial meditation at the present day. One of the most characteristic and popular tendencies of our time is that which prompts us to place confidence in the natural impulses of mankind, or, as the phrase runs, of humanity, and to believe in the continuous progress of society. Now the Christian, above all men, has a right, subject to some grave qualifications, to view with hope the course of history and of human development, because he believes that a Divine hand is guiding it, and that a Divine Spirit is present to convince men, more and more, ' of sin, of righteousness and of judgment.' But the amazing facts now in question seem to show that, apart from that guidance, there is no justification for such confidence in the natural instincts of mankind, and no such hope in humanity itself. The matter has been put to the test of experiment, and the result was the commission of the greatest crime the world has ever seen. Perfect truth and righteousness were brought before men, exhibited in flesh and blood, under the most favourable circumstances, and the result was that human nature rejected them. That is the bare and indisputable fact, and its lesson is unmistakeable. The surmise of Plato has been established, by this experience, as an unquestionable truth. There was an occasion when Light, absolute Light, came into the world; but men loved darkness rather than light, and did their utmost to extinguish the illumination, or, as in the example of Pilate, were indifferent to its extinction.

The cross must thus be regarded as an exhibition of human nature—of the nature which we all share—on the one hand rising up in rebellion against the Incarnation of Truth and Goodness, and on the other exhibiting a complete indifference to truth and justice as compared with the gratification of selfish comfort and with ease in this world. It was the malice of the Jew on the one side, and the indifference and levity of the Gentile on the other, by which our Lord was brought to the Cross. That Cross thus stands for ever, through all time and eternity, the witness to the true nature and consequence of sin—not by any arbitrary estimate, but by the invincible and indisputable evidence of actual experience. To this it was that man actually did come under the reign of nature, and law and philosophy. All the circumstances of ignominy, insult, and cruelty, which were heaped upon our blessed Lord, recoil in shame upon human nature, and are the standing condemnation of all our evil. To spurn everything that is good and true and pure, to insult and to murder the one man who embodied in Himself this truth and purity—this was shown by experience to be the natural working out of human evil, even under the guidance of a divinely instituted law, and under the authority of a representative of the highest pagan civilization.

But now let us pass on to enquire what must, by the nature of the case, be the attitude of God, not merely towards the particular crime then committed, but towards the moral evil of which it was the natural development? Could it be other than that of which the Scriptures speak, an attitude of hostility and of wrath, in the absence of some satisfaction for violations of His laws, of so heinous and deadly a character? It is certainly very strange that in these days there should be such hesitation, as there often is, in admitting this necessity. In the present day we have been taught more and more the inflexible and stern character of natural laws, when not interfered with, as at the time of the Gospel, by supernatural agency. We have come to understand that we are surrounded on all sides by a mass of physical laws which, in the ordinary course of things, exact payment, as it were, for every offence against them, to the uttermost farthing. They take no account of excuses on the ground of ignorance or even of good intentions. They avenge themselves, regardless of persons, of circumstances, and of consequences, upon all who violate or even neglect them. Nor is this true only of the laws of physical nature. We apprehend more and more that it is also true of social laws. The laws of political economy, the principles which govern trade and commerce, have their unbending operation. This unbending and irresistible character of law is one of the deepest convictions of our time; it is impressed on us more and more every day by every fresh discovery, and it has doubtless enlarged and elevated, in some important respects, our conception of the Divine nature and attributes. But is it to be supposed that, while the laws instituted by God to govern the action of inanimate matter are thus immutable and certain, and assert and avenge themselves, the laws He has instituted for the government of our moral nature are less immutable, and will be maintained by Him with less firmness? May we not apply in this connection our Lord's own illustration, and enquire whether, if He asserts with unwavering firmness the laws which regulate the growth of the flowers of the field, or cause the death of a sparrow, He will vindicate with less strictness those which He has laid down for the government of human hearts and wills? Surely, if there be any comparison between the two, the reverse must be the case. In proportion as spiritual and moral interests are greater than those of merely physical nature, in proportion as such awful scenes as those we are contemplating transcend, in their momentous import, any physical manifestations whatever, in that proportion must the justice of God be bound to assert the immutability and the operative force of His moral laws, with a solemnity vastly transcending His assertion of physical laws.

Men sometimes say of other laws, and of their consequences, that they are founded in the nature of things; but of the moral laws, we feel we have a right to say, without hesitation, that they are founded in the Divine nature itself. Righteousness, truth, and purity are manifestations of the essence of the Divine character; they are God's will, not in the sense of being determined by the choice of His wisdom for certain finite and temporary ends, but because they are one with Himself, and are as eternally necessary as He is. The heavens are the work of His fingers, and the physical laws which maintain them in their place are the rules which His wisdom has devised for that special purpose. 'In the beginning He laid the foundation of the earth, and the heavens are the works of His hands;' but the Psalmist contrasts them, in all their apparent stability, with the eternity of God Himself: 'They shall perish, but thou remainest; and they all shall wax old as doth a garment; and as a vesture shalt Thou fold them up, and they shall be changed; but Thou art the same, and Thy years shall not fail.' He is the same, ever loving righteousness and hating iniquity. He *is* Love, and He *is* Light. Other ordinances we may conceive being changed by a decree of His omnipotence, but the laws of right and wrong He cannot alter, because He cannot alter Himself.

With what jealousy then, as the Scriptures express it, must He not uphold among the creatures whom He has made in His image these moral and spiritual laws, in the obedience of which they chiefly resemble Him! If they are violated, is it not evident that it would be contrary to the deepest principles of the Divine nature to leave the violation without some conspicuous punishment—some vindication adequate to the depth and intensity of the evil which such violation involves? It may be permissible to observe, in passing, that in proportion as we realize this truth, shall we be in a position to apprehend the justice and necessity of those terrible punishments which, by God's command, were from time to time inflicted, in the course of His education of His chosen people, for heinous violations of the moral laws; such, for instance, as the extermination of the Canaanites. It is, too probably, because we are deficient in that moral indignation, that righteous wrath, which is an essential constituent in a perfectly righteous character, that such instances of Divine justice occasion us perplexity. If you regard people like the Canaanites as merely in an imperfect stage of morality, the judgment pronounced on them may appear harsh. But if, in accordance with St. Paul's teaching in the first chapter of the Epistle to the Romans, they are to be regarded as offending, in consequence of repeated neglect of the dictates of their conscience, against the eternal principles of the moral law, and as thus being in antagonism to the very essence of the character of God Himself, we shall not feel it difficult to understand that it was necessary for the intensity of that antagonism to be revealed and avenged.

If, in fact, we contemplate on a large scale this necessary relation of God to sinful man, this necessary relation of the Divine righteousness to evil, our marvel will be, not that in particular instances the indignation of God against moral evil has been expressed in terrible punishments, but that He has endured human evil with such longsuffering and patience, and that His moral laws, the most momentous of all, have not produced more overwhelming misery to the race which for so many centuries has violated them. There is a fine passage in the first book of Hooker's 'Ecclesiastical Polity,' in which he describes the momentous importance to men of the observance of natural laws. 'If nature,' he says, 'should intermit her course, and leave altogether, though it were but for a while, the observation of her own laws; if those principal and mother elements of the world, whereof all things in this lower world are made, should lose the qualities which now they have; if the frame of that heavenly arch erected over our heads should loosen and dissolve itself; if celestial spheres should forget their wonted motions, and by irregular volubility turn themselves any way as it might happen ; if the prince of the lights of heaven, which now as a giant doth run his unwearied course, should as it were through a languishing faintness begin to stand and to rest himself; if the moon should wander from her beaten way, the times and seasons of the year blend themselves by disordered and confused mixture, the winds breathe out their last gasp, the clouds yield no rain, the earth be defeated of heavenly influence, ... what would become of man himself, whom these things now do all serve? See we not plainly that obedience of creatures unto the law of nature is the stay of the whole world?' But see we not as plainly, that if such would be the necessary and terrible consequences of the disobedience of physical things to the law of nature, similar and more awful must be the natural consequences of the disobedience of moral beings to the law of right and wrong? This description of the disorganization of the physical frame of nature has but to be transferred to the moral world, in order to give an account, only too true, of that which has been the actual condition of human nature, as a whole, from the day of the fall until now. Our moral nature has intermitted her course, and has left, not merely for a while, but continuously, the observation of her own laws. The principal and mother elements of our moral constitution have been corrupted, and have lost the qualities with which they were endued; the frame of that heavenly arch erected in our souls, and revealing the will of God, has been loosened and dissolved; our conscience, that prince of the lights of the moral world, has languished and grown faint in an ineffectual struggle with human perversity; our passions and affections have blended themselves by disordered and confused mixture, until our earth has been 'defeated' of its most necessary heavenly influences. Can it be ascribed to anything but the mercy and longsuffering of God, to His gracious resolve that He would not allow the whole consequences of our evil to fall on us, that human nature, amidst its utter moral confusion, has escaped complete misery, degradation, and ruin? St. Paul does not hesitate to say so. 'The times of this ignorance,' he says, 'God winked at.' He exercises His omnipotence to reserve His judgments to the uttermost, and to give men time for repentance. But, unless all the principles of God's government were to be undermined, and the whole analogy of His dealings were to be falsified—if His moral laws were to possess any real and effectual sanction, some vindication they must have, one which should be at least as conspicuous, as awful, and prominent, in the moral sphere, as is the constant vindication of His other laws in the physical and social universe.

Now the chief truth embodied in the doctrine of the Atonement is that this vindication has been afforded by the Passion and Death of our Lord; and although, as has been already said, no theory on this subject has fathomed, or is likely to fathom, its deep mysteries, we can hardly be wrong in observing, as a matter of fact, one important respect in which that vindication was exhibited by the awful events we have been considering. We have seen that our Lord's death was the natural consequence, the inevitable working out, of human evil, when brought into contact with truth, righteousness, and purity. Had men been left to themselves, this is the result to which they would have come; they would have trampled out the truth and goodness which is the life of their souls, and God must needs have abandoned them, in the necessary vindication of His laws, to all the misery which they inflicted on our Saviour. But in enduring that misery, our Lord has exhibited once for all, to earth and to heaven, to time and to eternity, what is the natural consequence of the violation of God's moral laws. By suffering the extremity of misery, in soul and body, on the tree, He has manifested to the world the consequences of human sin—the consequences which in God's justice it must produce, if left to itself—as fully, as terribly, as vividly, as if the human race as a whole had themselves suffered such extremities. Nothing could be more horrible, nothing could be a more fearful manifestation of the deadly evil of sin, than that the holy and perfect and gentle Lord Jesus, who did no sin, neither was guile found in His mouth, should be betrayed and insulted, and tortured and crucified, and cast out of the world as one of its malefactors. It is sin which on the cross is crucified, and exposed to the scorn and hatred of men and angels. Nay, surely it is a more awful exhibition of the evil of sin that it should bring this suffering upon one so holy and innocent, than that it should simply have been left to work out the just judgment of those who were guilty. It is so fearful a curse, so awful a disease, that it involves not merely the guilty, it inflicts its terrible penalties not only on those who themselves have done wrong; but when the Son of God Himself takes human flesh for the salvation of mankind, it must needs bring its fearful consequences upon Him, and inflict on Him the worst sufferings which man can endure. All this, as has been said, is not by an arbitrary arrangement, not by any formal convention, as it were. God left men for a while to the consequences of their own evil acts, and permitted His Son to appear among them, and the moral laws He had established vindicated themselves, by their violation working itself out into this fearful crime and cruelty.

In short, what do these events prove, but that men, if left to themselves, could have gone on in no other course than that of extirpating from among themselves more and more every grace, every truth, and every virtue for which they were designed? That which they did to goodness incarnate, they must have done to goodness wherever it appeared. Their very curse, the natural expression of the wrath of God against their sins, would be that those sins should be left to develop their hateful fruit, until it issued in utter moral corruption. As they did not like to retain God in their knowledge, God gave them over to a reprobate mind, or, as the same method of the divine judgment is expressed in the Psalms, He gave them up unto their own heart's lusts, and let them follow their own imaginations. Had our Lord been simply a perfect man, His death would still have been the example and the prophecy of the uprising of human nature against all things that are just and true and pure, against everything, in a word, that is precious in life. And thus by the exercise of the very passions which put Him to death, men must have gone on revenging their sins upon themselves, until they had made human society a hell upon earth. This would have been the natural and inevitable operation of the Divine judgment upon them; and by no other natural means could the righteousness of God have been fully manifested. If we could suppose God interposing by some act of arbitrary power to create men afresh, as it were, and to blot out the consequences of their sins, it would have amounted to a practical declaration that the moral law could be readily dispensed with, and the eternal supremacy of righteousness would have been superseded. But on the other hand, if that eternal law had been left to work itself out, we see by its operation in bringing about the death of Christ that it must have wrought out the death of all righteousness and peace among mankind.

But here, far as our conceptions must needs fall short of a truth which appears to be the very centre of the Divine dealings with mankind, we may, perhaps, apprehend something of the mystery of the sacrifice of Christ. We perceive that the Son of God, by taking human flesh, allowed that inevitable consequence of the operation of the law of righteousness to be wrought on Himself. He endured that He should be cast out from among mankind; and if He had been one of themselves that rejection would have been irreparable. But He was more than the Son of Man; He was the Son of God; and though they thus cast Him out, their wicked effort, through His mercy, was ineffectual. He revealed to them, in His sufferings, what was the real nature of their sin and its consequences; and then, having thus satisfied the law of God by allowing it to work itself out to the full, He interceded with His Father for mercy towards us, and returned among us to save us, having obtained for us the remission of sins.

But this having been done, and done once for all, that vindication stands for ever, and we can at least see that it goes far to answer the main purposes of the actual infliction of punishment on the sinner.

God willed not the death of the sinner, but rather that he should return and repent. Provided His law is vindicated in such a way as to declare His righteousness, to make it manifest to the whole universe that He cannot be reconciled to evil, and at the same time to arouse in men a due hatred of evil and love of righteousness, He has no pleasure, but the contrary, in exacting the ultimate penalty of sin from every one of His feeble creatures; and He offers them forgiveness, on condition they submit themselves to His justice and His mercy, by seeking that forgiveness solely on the ground of the satisfaction which has been offered by our Lord. As long, indeed, as a man desires to stand by himself, and expects God to overlook his offences, as though they did not need any exemplary punishment. it may well be necessary, for his very salvation, that he should for a while be left in his sin and its misery, that he may learn the intense reality and terror of God's moral law. But if, by sheltering himself solely under the sacrifice of Christ, he does homage to God's righteousness, confessing that his evil and the evil of his fellows deserved, and must in the course of nature have received, an intolerable punishment, then may it become compatible with God's relation to such a soul, that He should pardon it, that He should stay the natural consequences of its moral evil, that He should bestow His Spirit on it, sanctify and save it. Again let me repeat, for fear of misapprehension, that the Atonement in its relation to man, no less than in its relation to God, must needs present aspects, and exert influences, which no single point of view can include. But so far as these considerations reach, they appear to show, in some measure, how the Passion of our Lord would, by its inherent moral efficacy, provide means of reconciliation between God and man. Far, in fact, as we must be from entering into the depth of the riches of the wisdom and mercy of God, and of our Lord Jesus Christ, which were manifested in the great sacrifice of the cross, do not these considerations serve to help us to realize at once the evil of sin, the grace of our Saviour in offering an atonement for it, and the justice of God, alike in demanding such a satisfaction for sin, in accepting that which was offered Him on the cross, and in pardoning those who believe in it? Is not this comprehensive manifestation of justice and mercy summed up in St. Paul's words, 'Whom God hath set forth to be a propitiation through faith in His blood, to declare His righteousness for the remission of sins that are past, through the forbearance of God; to declare, I say, at this time His righteousness: that He might be just, and the justifier of Him which believeth in Jesus?'

Let me add only one consideration, at once to

obviate one of the chief objections which are raised against this great doctrine, and to recall the deep obligation which it has created for us. It has been objected that this is a vicarious atonement, and that the innocent is made to suffer for the guilty. Now if it were a vicarious atonement by one of those arbitrary and artificial arrangements of which I have spoken, and if the innocent had been made to suffer for the guilty by the decree of God, against, or without, the will of the sufferer, such objections might apply. But it is an essential part of our Saviour's suffering for us that it is perfectly voluntary on His part. That it is so, depends on the cardinal doctrine of Christianity, that He is the Son of God, one in substance with the Father. As God, He saw perfectly the whole nature and consequences of the sin of man; He foresaw, as His agony in the garden shows, the whole bitterness of the cup which He had resolved to drink; and being one with the Father, and equal to Him as touching His Godhead, He of His perfect free will consented to lay aside the power and privileges of His Divine nature, and to be the victim in whom human sin should work out its terrible consequences. There is here no infliction of vicarious suffering on unresisting innocence. There is the deliberate and infinitely gracious resolve of one who was under no obligation, or none but that which His own perfect love created, to die that we might not die eternally, to suffer that we might be saved. Let us contemplate the Father and the Son thus working together for men's salvation—the Father sending the Son, and consenting that He should suffer all this misery and ignominy in human form, and the Son consenting to it, of His own original free will, for the vindication of His Father's law—and what do we behold but infinite love, co-operating with infinite justice, and establishing the intensest obligations on us for love in return that could possibly be conceived? Shall we not respond to the exhortation of the Apostle: 'Herein is love, not that we loved God, but that He loved us, and sent His Son to be the propitiation for our sins. . . . We love Him because He first loved us'—loved us in all our sin and misery, and gave His life to save us? Shall not 'the blood of Christ, who through the Eternal Spirit offered Himself without spot to God, purge our conscience from dead works to serve the living God?' Let us at least learn, from the contemplation of these awful consequences of human sin, the deep solemnity of that struggle between good and evil which is every day, and every hour, going forwards in our own hearts. Let us remember that whenever we are faithless to the dictates of our consciences, and disobedient to the voice of God within us, we are committing sins of precisely the same kind as those

L

which brought our Lord Jesus Christ to the cross. But that, on the other hand, in every word spoken, or deed done, or thought controlled, in obedience to righteousness and truth, we are rendering Him the one reward which He desires for His sufferings in our behalf. We are enabling Him, in some measure, ' to see of the travail of His soul, and to be satisfied.'

LECTURE VII

THE WITNESS TO OUR LORD'S RESURRECTION

"This Jesus hath God raised up, whereof we all are witnesses. Therefore being by the right hand of God exalted, and having received of the Father the promise of the Holy Ghost, He hath shed forth this, which ye now see and hear."—*Acts* ii. 32, 33.

THE glorious event celebrated on Whit-Sunday is the culminating point of the revelation of the New Testament. On the one hand it is the immediate result to which the life and death of our Lord were directed, and it is also the point from which the history of the Church takes its start. Until a comparatively recent date, it was the last of the great festivals of the Christian year; for it was not until the fourteenth century that the observance of Trinity Sunday was enjoined upon the Western Church. Accordingly Whit-Sunday casts its illumination upon all the sacred events which have been previously commemorated, and they are all to be interpreted by its light. More particularly will this be found to be the case with respect to the events we have been celebrating in the season just passed—those of the Resurrection and Ascension. The remarkable position which the great event of the day of Pentecost holds in this respect is sufficiently illustrated from the character of St. Peter's argument in the passage from which my text is taken. That argument was delivered on the day of Pentecost, and was the first public utterance of the Apostles since our Lord's death and resurrection. He had been with them forty days between His Resurrection and Ascension; and since then, in obedience to His command, they had been quietly waiting in Jerusalem. When they returned from witnessing the Ascension, they went into an upper room, and continued with one accord in prayer and supplication with the women, and Mary the Mother of Jesus, and with His brethren. There, and in this attitude of prayer and supplication, they waited for the promise of the Father, of which their Lord had spoken to them; taking no step whatever in pursuance of their commission as Apostles, except to complete the number of twelve chosen witnesses, by the election of Matthias into the room of Judas. But at the end of the ten days, on the great Jewish feast of Pentecost, the wonderful manifestation of spiritual power came upon them which we to-day commemorate. They were enabled to proclaim, in the various tongues spoken by the Jews then gathered in Jerusalem out of every nation under heaven, the wonderful works of God — doubtless the great facts of our Saviour's ministry, which had just been completed. Then it was, but not till then, that St. Peter opened to the Jewish people the gracious message with which he had been entrusted, respecting our Saviour's Ascension, and His exaltation to the right hand of God. Then was exhibited to the eyes of the Jews a marvellous exercise of new spiritual powers —a momentous fact which aroused amazement, and compelled men to say one to another, 'What meaneth this?' St. Peter comes forward to give the answer, and announces that this is the manifestation of the risen Christ. He reminds his hearers of the whole course of our Lord's ministry, and of its awful close: 'Jesus of Nazareth,' he said, 'a man approved of God among you by miracles and wonders and signs, which God did by Him in the midst of you, as ye yourselves also know: Him, being delivered by the determinate counsel and foreknowledge of God, ye have taken, and by wicked hands have crucified and slain: whom God hath raised up, having loosed the pains of death: because it was not possible that He should be holden of it. . . This Jesus hath God raised up, whereof we all are witnesses. Therefore being by the right hand of God exalted, and having received of the Father the promise of the Holy Ghost, He hath shed forth this, which ye now see and hear. . . . Therefore let all the house of Israel know assuredly, that God hath made that same Jesus, whom ye have crucified, both Lord and Christ.'

Such was the order and method of the first preaching of the Resurrection. The great event is proclaimed, in the first instance, not in itself, nor even in relation to the ministry and the death which had preceded it, but in relation to a new and great manifestation of spiritual power, and as explaining that manifestation. The Apostles are not commissioned to bear witness simply to the historical miracle that our Lord had risen from the grave, or even to the historic fact of His Ascension in glory. Their commission was to declare that He had risen in power, and that He was a living Saviour, bestowing the gifts of the Holy Ghost upon those who submitted themselves to Him. 'Repent,' he said, 'and be baptized every one of you in the name of Jesus Christ for the remission of sins, and ye shall receive the gift of the Holy Ghost.' The Resurrection, the Ascension, and the bestowal of the Holy Ghost are presented in such immediate relation to each other that it is difficult to distinguish them. 'This Jesus hath God raised up. . . Therefore, being by the right hand of God exalted, and having received of the Father the promise of the Holy Ghost, He hath shed forth this, which ye now see and hear.' The Resurrection, in short, is not proclaimed for its own sake, for the mere significance of the fact that our Lord had risen from the grave, but as involving the supreme fact of His having assumed a new, a mightier, and still more gracious life, and as being the giver of new spiritual powers. The proclamation is not merely that Christ did rise, but that Christ is risen; has assumed all power in heaven and earth, and is working spiritual miracles, even mightier than those He displayed when he was upon earth.

The same characteristic is to be observed in all the discourses and acts of St. Peter which follow. The next instance of which we read is the healing of the lame man, and St. Peter turns it to account as evidence of the presence and power of the living Saviour: 'Ye men of Israel, why marvel ye at this? or why look ye so earnestly on us, as though by our own power or holiness we had made this man to walk? . . The God of our fathers hath glorified His Son Jesus, whom ye delivered up. . . . Ye denied the Holy One and the Just, and desired a murderer to be granted unto you, and killed the Prince of Life, whom God hath raised from the dead; whereof we are witnesses. And His name through faith in His name hath made this man strong, whom ye see and know; yea, the faith which is by Him hath given him this perfect soundness in the presence of you all.' When summoned before the Council, St. Peter's reply is of precisely the same character: 'We ought to obey God rather than men. The God of our fathers raised up Jesus, whom ye slew and hanged on a tree. Him hath God exalted with His right hand to be a Prince and a Saviour, for to give repentance to Israel, and remission of sins. And we are His witnesses of these things; and so is also the Holy Ghost, whom God hath given to them that obey Him.' It was in this sense that, with great power, the Apostles gave witness of the resurrection of the Lord Jesus, 'and great grace was upon them all;' 'and many wonders and signs were done by the Apostles.' Similarly the culminating point of St. Stephen's testimony was that he saw the heavens opened, and the Son of Man standing on the right hand of God. So also the appearance of our Lord to St. Paul is the revelation to him of a living Christ—risen, not only in the sense of having been raised from the grave, but of being present, and exercising supernatural powers. In all cases, it is from actual present facts that the proclamation of the Resurrection starts— from the amazing fact of the descent of the Holy Ghost; from the evidence of the power exercised by the name of Christ over the bodies and souls of men; or from actual manifestations of the risen Lord. In a word, it is not to a past, but to a present fact, that the testimony of the Apostles is born; its object is to interpret present realities, and to bring men into the enjoyment of new powers.

Now this is a consideration which appears to throw

light upon the nature of the evidence for the Resurrection on the one hand, and upon our present relation to that great truth on the other. It will be seen, in the first place, that the witness of the Apostles did not rest simply upon their assertions respecting what they alone had seen; it was not simply that they, and they only, had found the grave empty, and that our Lord had appeared to them, and had subsequently ascended to heaven. Had that been all they had to say, it might not have been difficult for the enemies of our Lord to have either described them as mere enthusiasts, or to have charged them with deception, as in the story, which St. Matthew tells us was set on foot, of the disciples having stolen away our Lord's body while the soldiers slept. The testimony of twelve unlearned and ignorant men, despised as the followers of a crucified master, would scarcely, if it had stood alone and unsupported, have found credence for so great a miracle. At all events, the Apostles did not proclaim this testimony as long as it stood alone. When they proclaim it, they are able to appeal to a present fact, to a number of successive facts, which verify it. They are suddenly endued with new spiritual powers; in the name of the Lord Jesus they work miracles on the bodies of men, and convert thousands to repentance and to a holy life; and it is with the support of these facts, and in order to explain them, that they declare what they had seen and heard of our Lord after His resurrection. They thus offer a practical attestation of their message of the strongest possible kind. They proclaim to the Jews that Christ is living; and here, they say, is the proof of it, that the Holy Spirit is bestowed on us, that miracles are wrought in His name; that He actually gives power, both spiritual and bodily, to those who believe on Him. This it was, and not mere testimony to the past, which produced so great an effect in Jerusalem, and which so alarmed the Jewish rulers. The Apostles, in a word, spoke of a present reality; that reality was verified by present experience, and they thus established a most weighty claim to be believed on their explanation of it. If the name of Jesus, through faith in Him, had, as a matter of fact, made men whole in soul and body, then there was every reason to believe the witnesses who appealed to that name, and who stated facts which would explain the power it exerted.

This consideration, perhaps, will help to explain one point in the Evangelical narratives of the Resurrection which might otherwise seem a little surprising. I mean their comparative brevity, and the lack of the circumstantial character which marks some other portions of the sacred narrative. There can be no doubt that the Resurrection occupies the most prominent place in the preaching of the

Apostles, both at the outset and throughout the Epistles. The grand message of the Acts of the Apostles is that of a risen Christ, whether it be in the mouth of St. Peter or St. Paul. But, nevertheless, the circumstances of the Passion are narrated by the Evangelists with far more particularity than those of the Resurrection. The narratives of the Passion occupy a very considerable space, but those of the Resurrection occupy in St. Matthew, St. Mark, and St. Luke only one chapter, and in the two former but very brief ones. In St. John two chapters are devoted to the subject; but one of them is mainly the account of a special incident in our Lord's intercourse with His disciples after the Resurrection; and the account of the Resurrection itself is of the same brief character as that in the other Evangelists. This feature in the narratives has been made a ground of objection to the belief they proclaim, and it is urged that we ought to have been furnished with more detailed and circumstantial relations of an event of such supreme importance. But this objection springs from the supposition—a supposition unconsciously admitted too often by Christians themselves—that the actual rising from the grave, the mere fact of our Lord not having seen corruption, is the main fact to be substantiated. Sceptical writers, in dealing with the subject, fasten attention exclusively on this feature in it; they make it an objection that no eye-witness had borne testimony to the resurrection itself—that no one actually saw our Saviour rise. They argue, in short, as if it were simply a past fact and an isolated one, with which we have to deal; and they complain that the Apostles and other disciples took no sufficient pains to afford satisfaction to the legitimate and necessary enquiries, which the report of so extraordinary an occurrence must occasion. But the Evangelists, it will now be seen, approached the question from a very different point of view. The mere fact of our Saviour having left the grave was but a part, and comparatively a small part, in their view of the Resurrection. The essential part of the Resurrection was our Lord's re-appearance to His disciples in glorious form, and the fact that He was still living, as a Prince and Saviour to them. But of this great fact believers were assured, not only by the Apostles' report of His appearance to them, but by the daily evidences they had of His living power and grace. The fact of his having risen was in great measure substantiated to them by the most conspicuous records of early Christian life, and by their own experience. The events narrated in the Acts of the Apostles proved that the Lord was with His Church, and this fact was to them the most certain of all realities. The Evangelists did not write, therefore, to prove the Resurrection. They wrote under the living conviction of the Resurrection being true; and they were only concerned to give such details of it as might suit their particular purpose.

With respect to the differences in their narration, some interesting observations have been made in a valuable book on the resurrection of Our Lord, recently published by Dr. Milligan, the Professor of Divinity in the University of Aberdeen.* He observes that the different Evangelists seem to present the Resurrection of Our Lord in a light corresponding to that in which they had treated His whole previous life. Thus he points out that St. Matthew, having been occupied with the Galilean ministry, as that in which he beheld the fulfilment of Old Testament prophecy, and having, throughout the whole of his Gospel, set forth Jesus as the bringer in of a true righteousness, as the great lawgiver of the New Testament economy, seems to have these thoughts mainly in his mind when he comes to the Resurrection. He is chiefly occupied with the appearances in Galilee; and the idea of the lawgiver, the author of the Sermon on the Mount, may be traced in those words of the risen Lord which St. Matthew alone has preserved, 'Go ye, therefore, and teach all nations, ... teaching them to observe

---

* *The Resurrection of our Lord.* By William Milligan, D.D., Professor of Divinity and Biblical Criticism in the University of Aberdeen. London, 1881, pp. 59–61.

all things whatsoever I have commanded you.' Thus it is that in the closing verses of St. Mark's Gospel we find particulars and words of the risen Lord which at once recall to us that mighty march of His power, with which we have been made familiar by the Gospel as a whole. Thus it is that St. Luke, who had especially set forth the human Saviour, and the universality of His mission of forgiveness, seizes on those circumstances in connection with His Resurrection which illustrate the same points. The story of the disciples at Emmaus brings Him before us vividly as what He had always been, the human friend; and St. Luke alone speaks—not as St. Matthew, of teaching all the nations—but of repentance and remission of sins to be preached to all; and he alone tells us of the consolatory blessing with which, lifting up His hands, the Lord blessed His disciples when He ascended to Heaven. Finally, it is thus that St. John, who has been occupied throughout his Gospel with the manifestation of Our Lord's glory, fixes on particular circumstances respecting the risen Lord which illustrate the same truth. The manifestations of which he speaks are related less for the purpose of convincing us that the Lord had risen, than for the sake of illustrating the nature of His risen state, and the manner in which one of the loftiest confessions of the Gospel was drawn forth by it—'my Lord and my God.'

From this point of view, it will be seen how unreasonable is the stress which has been laid on the fact of the absence from one or two old manuscripts of the last verses of St. Mark's Gospel.* It must be observed that, independently of those verses, St. Mark bears emphatic witness to the Resurrection, for that testimony is borne in the first eight verses of his last chapter, which are not doubted. But even if it were the case that the last verses did not belong to the Gospel—and they are defended by scholars of very diverse views—it would still be inconceivable that their absence should affect, in the slightest degree, the evidence for the Resurrection. The belief of the Church in that event dates from a few days, or, we might say, hours, after the crucifixion, and St. Peter, at whose instance, and by whose guidance, St. Mark wrote, would certainly have been the first to insist on the great fact. If, therefore, any conclusion were to be drawn from the absence of these verses in certain manuscripts, it could not, with any reason, be that the main circumstances narrated in them were doubtful, but, on the contrary, that they were so certain, that no special attention was paid to the narrative which contained them.

---

* For practical purposes, from only one; for this leaf of the Sinaitic MS. is in the handwriting of the Scribe of the Vatican MS. See Tischendorf, *Nov. Test. Vatic.* p. xxii.

But however this may be, the one point on which the other Gospels are agreed in insisting is that our Lord, after rising from the dead, claimed absolute power in heaven and in earth. 'All power,' He says in St. Matthew, 'is given unto me in heaven and in earth. Go ye therefore, and teach all nations, baptizing them in the name of the Father, and of the Son, and of the Holy Ghost: teaching them to observe all things whatsoever I have commanded you: and, lo, I am with you alway, even unto the end of the world.' So in St. Luke—'Thus it is written, and thus it behoved Christ to suffer, and to rise from the dead the third day: and that repentance and remission of sins should be preached in His name among all nations.' So St. John, 'These things are written, that ye might believe that Jesus is the Christ, the Son of God; and that believing ye might have life through His name.' In view of this great fact, that the Lord was actually living, and that they were in communion with Him, the details of the occurrences which attended his Resurrection were of secondary importance. 'Why seek ye the living among the dead?' said the angels, 'He is not here, but is risen;' and accordingly the thoughts of the Evangelists turn at once from the tomb and from all the minor details on which modern curiosity would dwell, and pass at once to our Lord's risen and glorious life. Enough is told by each Evangelist to afford a general conception of the character of the event, and to illustrate the particular purpose with which he writes; but we pass rapidly from the crucified to the glorified Lord. We are made to feel that the point of importance consists in the fact that He is now in glory and power, not in the mere incidents by which He passed from humiliation to glory. The details of His Passion were of infinite importance as a solemn act of the past, done once for all. But the important point respecting His Resurrection was not that He once rose, but that He was now risen, and alive for evermore; and upon this, in accordance with their usual reserve on points of secondary detail, the Evangelists are content mainly to insist.

There is, in fact, a great deficiency, or even fallacy, in a fine image which has been used on this subject. It has been said that the church of Christ was built over an empty tomb. But it is not, and never was, the empty grave upon which the faith of the Apostles, and the life of the church, was founded. It was the existence of our Saviour in glory, and, more than that, His actual energy and life-giving power, through His Spirit, which gave the Church its foundation, and built up its members as living stones into a holy temple. It is here, accordingly, that the real controversy lies at the present day with respect to the events we have been considering.

Modern controversy has led to two remarkable admissions on the part of the most determined opponents of the Christian creed—one that there is no doubt the grave of our Lord was empty on the resurrection morning; the other, that the disciples of our Lord were thoroughly and honestly convinced that their Master had risen from the dead. What is alleged is that, however the removal of our Lord's body may be accounted for, the belief in His resurrection may be explained by the theory of visions and phantasms. But all these evasions are shattered against the solid facts to which this day bears witness. The disciples, we have seen, did not yield to the impulse, to which mere visions would have led them, to proclaim simply our Lord's deliverance from the grave. They waited quietly for ten days after His last disappearance from them, and then they appealed to the patent fact of His exercising a new and living power. As an historic event, the deliverance of our Lord from the grave would have been, no doubt, of profound and momentous significance; but it would not have been the reality upon which Christians lived. It was not merely, in a word, belief in the resurrection, but belief in a risen and living Christ which was, and is, the corner stone of the Christian edifice.

For instance, Baur says that 'the question as to the nature and the reality of the resurrection lies outside the sphere of historical enquiry. For the purposes of historical considerations we must be content with the simple fact that in the faith of the disciples, the Resurrection of Jesus came to be regarded as a solid and irrefragable certainty. It was in this faith that Christianity acquired a firm basis for its historic development. What history requires, as the necessary antecedent of all that is to follow, is not so much the fact of the Resurrection of Jesus, but rather the belief that it was a fact.'* This view of Baur, so far as Christianity is concerned, is accepted by Strauss, though he cannot similarly restrain himself from enquiring into the origin of the belief. But not only is it necessary to enquire into the origin of the belief; it is necessary to consider how the belief came to be something far more than Baur thus represents. Was it the case, or was it not, that, as St. Peter declared on the day of Pentecost, new powers, new spiritual and moral forces, were introduced into the world, and that the lives of those who believed in Christ were transformed? Baur rejects the authenticity of the Acts of the Apostles; but, as was shown in the second lecture of this course, he is not followed in this even by some of his own disciples; and M. Renan pronounces unquestionably in favour of the authen-

* *Das Christenthum und die Christliche Kirche der drei ersten Jahrhunderte;* Tübingen, 1853, p. 39.

ticity of the Acts. But if they are true, then, as we have urged, the facts of the day of Pentecost are to be accounted for as much as the open grave; and St. Peter's account of them is the only one which meets the case.

But with respect to this whole theory of the excitement and visionary tendencies of the Apostles and of the early Church, I will ask you to follow me for a few moments in contemplating a picture of that Church, and of the apostolic mind which guided it, drawn by the hand, as cannot reasonably be doubted, of the very Apostle upon whose utterances on the day of Pentecost we have been meditating. The first Epistle of St. Peter is brought before us by the Church in the services of the recent season, and it presents a striking picture of the tone of Christian life, and of the relation of that life to the great events we have been considering. It starts from a description of the manifold trials which the Christians had to endure, passing through a fire of tribulation, and supported by the lively hope of a future salvation through the resurrection of Jesus Christ. Their faith, thus tried by fire, would be found unto praise and honour and glory at His appearing. On Him their hopes and thoughts were centred, 'Whom, having not seen, they loved; in Whom, though now they saw Him not, yet believing, they rejoiced with joy unspeakable and full of glory, receiving the end of their faith, even the salvation of their souls.' Their spiritual life was being daily deepened and developed, and as living stones they were being built up a spiritual house, a holy priesthood, to offer up spiritual sacrifices to God through Jesus Christ. Here, as in the similar picture drawn by St. James, there is no excitement, none of that extreme enthusiasm to which the phenomena of the early Christian Church have been often ascribed. On the contrary, the Apostle bids his readers to pass the time of their sojourning here in fear, remembering at how vast a price their spiritual blessings had been bought, that they were not redeemed with corruptible things, as silver and gold, from their vain conversation received by tradition from their fathers, but with the precious blood of Christ. Their lively hope of an inheritance incorruptible and undefiled, and that fadeth not away, reserved in heaven for them, is not to exalt them or excite them, but, on the contrary, to impress them with a solemn and awful apprehension of the great trust conferred upon them, and of the terrible consequences of their faithlessness to it. They must gird up the loins of their minds, be sober, obedient, guileless, abstaining from fleshly lusts, submitting themselves to every ordinance of man for the Lord's sake; as free, but not as using their liberty for a cloak of maliciousness, but as the servants of God; honouring all men, loving the brotherhood, fearing God, and honouring the King. They are to be ready to give an answer to every man who asks them a reason of the hope that is in them, in meekness and fear. The meekness of Christ is to be ever in their thoughts; and forasmuch as He had suffered for them in the flesh, they are to arm themselves likewise with the same mind. The whole epistle, in short, is but an expansion of the exhortation, 'Be sober and watch unto prayer, and above all things have fervent charity among yourselves.' Such was the spirit, and such the whole energy of the early Church, wherever it was undisturbed by controversy, and its thoughts could be concentrated upon the growth of the spiritual life.

Whether as an incidental evidence for the truth of the New Testament history, or for the purposes of our practical instruction, there is scarcely anything more remarkable than the juxtaposition of ideas thus presented to us. The Ascension of Christ was the culminating point of our Saviour's manifested glory. His Resurrection had been a glorious manifestation of His greatness. He was declared, says St. Paul, to be the Son of God with power, according to the Spirit of holiness, by the Resurrection from the dead. After His Resurrection He was surrounded by an atmosphere of majesty and mysterious power. He was visibly superior to the ordinary conditions and limitations of human life, and there was that about Him which inspired the Apostles with an abiding sense of awe in His presence. But his Ascension, interpreted to them by angelic messengers, was at once recognized by them as bespeaking His assumption of inconceivable glory. It would be doing great injustice to the noble conceptions with which the minds of Jews like the Apostles were familiar, to suppose that by the heaven, into which they understood Him to have ascended, they meant no more than the mere physical firmament. When He said to Nicodemus 'No man hath ascended up to heaven but He that came down from heaven, even the Son of Man which is in heaven,' He was at once understood to be speaking of that secret place, that holy of holies, which God Himself inhabited. 'Go to my brethren,' He had said, 'and say unto them, I ascend unto my Father and your Father, unto my God and your God.' 'The heaven is my throne,' saith the Lord, 'and the earth is my footstool.' Accordingly, the Epistle to the Hebrews speaks of our 'great High Priest that hath passed into the heavens,' 'made higher than the heavens;' and St. Paul says that 'He that descended is the same also that ascended up far above all heavens.' In short, the word heaven has various meanings in Scripture. But judged by all the associations of the word when applied to our Lord's Ascension, it is evident that the Apostles, from the first, gave it the very loftiest signification. Whatever heaven was higher than all the rest, whatever sanctuary was holier than all which are called holies, whatever place was deemed of the greatest dignity in the courts above, there and unto that presence did they believe our Saviour to have entered. Thenceforth, as this Epistle of St. Peter bears witness, their whole thoughts and affections were centred upon Him in His glory. They looked to Him for all grace and favour, and they waited patiently for His full revelation hereafter. But now let us observe by what means and in what circumstances they conceived that they were maintaining communion with Him and sharing His glory. With such magnificent conceptions of His greatness, it would not have seemed unnatural if they had been absorbed in some ecstatic visions, and had been carried away by spiritual excitement. The visible glory of the Ascension, the angelic message, the occasional gifts of miraculous power, the descent of the Holy Ghost, and the spiritual endowments conferred upon them, might all have tended to produce in them such a mood of exaltation. But the effect is precisely the reverse. That which is aroused in them is the deepest humility, patience, simplicity, and submission to trials and temptations. There were moments when some Apostles, like St. Paul, might be caught up into the third heaven, and hear unspeakable words, not lawful for a man to utter. But, for the most part, Apostles and ordinary Christians alike found in the Saviour's Ascension, and in the visions of glory which it opened to them, only a stimulus and support in the humblest and most modest duties.

This result is perhaps mainly due to the consideration of the complete continuity which existed between the Saviour's life on earth and His existence in heaven. 'This same Jesus,' said the angels, 'which is taken up from you into heaven, shall so come in like manner as ye have seen Him go into heaven;' and similarly their thoughts were always carried back to that same Jesus as He had lived and died among them. They could not see Him now, as St. Peter says; but they had seen Him, and had companied with Him during His ministry. They had seen and had heard all His humiliation, His meekness and His patience, and they recurred to this as to an experience in which they could be sure of being one with Him and sharing His real glory. The Jesus who was exalted was the suffering Jesus, the man of sorrows and acquainted with grief, and it was the truth and patience of His life which they contemplated as now exalted. His human life was not, so to speak, an accident of His existence, which had been laid aside, as a thing to be forgotten, after His exaltation. It had remained, and must always remain, an essential part of His experience, an indispensable element in His nature. Hereafter they hoped to share the glory upon which He had entered; but for the present, while upon earth, as He had been, they could chiefly be one with Him in those humble graces of which He had been so perfect an exemplar. It is thus impossible to separate any one part of the mind of the Apostles from the rest. He that ascended is the same also that descended, and the very depths of earth are thus united to the loftiest heights of heaven. Thus it is that one part of the New Testament supports the others, that the Gospels, the Acts of the Apostles, and the Epistles combine to produce one harmonious result. Consider them separately, and they may be difficult of comprehension; but read them united, and the story they tell of the Incarnation, the Passion, the Resurrection, and the spiritual life of the Church after the gift of the Holy Spirit, exhibits a complete unity.

These considerations enable us to close this lecture with some thoughts which may help us to rise above controversy, and which may be a support to us in many a difficulty of faith. We have seen that St. Peter's faith in the Resurrection was not simply faith in a past event, but was faith in the living Lord who had risen and ascended, and who now bestows all grace upon His people.

His appeal to the Jews was built alike on the past and on the present, and the present was as important an element in it as the past. It may be the same to ourselves. Of course, if the historic reality of the events narrated in the Gospels could be disproved, we should have to reconsider our position altogether; and it is hard to see what would remain of the beliefs and convictions which so many generations of Christians have held dear. But there is no such disproof; and on the other hand we possess—every Christian should possess in his own experience—a conviction, not less clear than that to which St. Peter appealed, of the living power and life of our risen and ascended Lord. After all, there is this permanent evidence to the truth of our Lord's Resurrection, and to His present glory and power, that all Christians, and the Church at large, can approach Him by prayer, and receive from Him a grace and power, of which they may be as assured as of any other fact in their experience, to enable them continually to realize in increasing degree the graces of the spiritual life. In proportion as we realize this privilege, will our path be untroubled by the shadows of doubt, and shall we be enabled to bear witness to others of the power of the Lord's Resurrection.

LECTURE VIII

OUR LORD'S RETURN TO JUDGMENT

"And while they looked stedfastly towards heaven as He went up, behold, two men stood by them in white apparel; which also said, Ye men of Galilee, why stand ye gazing up into heaven? This same Jesus, which is taken up from you into heaven, shall so come in like manner as ye have seen Him go into heaven."—*Acts* i. 10, 11.

It must at least confirm our faith in those angelic manifestations which are narrated in the New Testament to observe how profound is the significance on each occasion of the utterances of the heavenly messengers. The name of Jesus, with the assurance that 'He shall save His people from their sins,' has, from the moment it was uttered till the present day, embodied the sum and substance of the Gospel. The song of the multitude of the heavenly host near Bethlehem, 'Glory to God in the highest, and on earth peace, good will towards men,' has been similarly felt, at all times, to express the essential glory of the Christian dispensation. The clear and calm gaze of heaven seems to penetrate to the heart of the great mystery it contemplates, and the central truth is presented to our meditation in one pregnant phrase. The same characteristic marks the utterance of the angels to the Apostles on the occasion of the Ascension. There is something intensely natural and vivid in the description of the Apostles looking stedfastly towards heaven as He went up—all their hearts and minds yearning after their Lord, lately restored to them from the grave, with whom they had lived in sacred communion for forty days, and now suddenly vanishing from them into those mysterious depths. At that moment angelic voices recall them to earth and to the realities around them, and tell them what is the chief significance, for the practical purposes of life, of the event they were witnessing. That which it was of supreme importance for them to realize and keep in mind was, that the Lord who had thus left them would return, the same in nature, in character, and in power— 'This same Jesus, which is taken up from you into heaven, shall so come in like manner as ye have seen Him go into heaven.' All their life was to be controlled by this belief; their thoughts were ever to look forward to that great day. He had ascended into heaven and had assumed His seat of power and judgment at the right hand of the Father, and He would hereafter return to execute that judgment visibly, in human form, and with the human as well as divine authority with which they were familiar. Thus, at the very moment of the Ascension, the thoughts of the disciples were directed by heavenly guidance to the future return of our Lord to establish his kingdom finally, and to execute judgment; and in accordance with this direction, the creed of the Church has ever combined the two truths in intimate connection. 'He ascended into heaven, and sitteth on the right hand of God the Father Almighty: from thence He shall come to judge the quick and the dead.'

That the last angelic words uttered respecting our Lord's work and office, at the moment of His departure, should thus point us forward to His future return to judge the world, is a fact of deep and manifold significance; and it merits our attention the more at the present day, by reason of the vivid light it casts upon some of the most conspicuous of our perplexities and controversies. For its due appreciation it is important to bear in mind how exactly this final angelic message corresponds with the whole tenour of our Lord's ministry and teaching. We are told that His preaching was from the first summed up in the message, 'Repent, for the kingdom of heaven is at hand;' and, although that proclamation has a double aspect—of salvation no less than of judgment—the aspect of judgment would seem to be the primary one. Such, certainly, was its meaning in the mouth of John the Baptist. He explained his proclamation to mean that One was coming after him whose fan was in His hand, who would throughly purge His floor, and gather His wheat into the garner, but who would burn up the chaff with unquenchable fire. That this meaning, indeed, was prominent in our Lord's proclamation of the kingdom of heaven is forcibly illustrated by the Sermon on the Mount. To regard that Sermon as simply a collection of maxims of morality is to miss its most distinctive characteristic—that characteristic which aroused the astonishment of those to whom it was spoken—its tone of authority. It not only proclaims moral duties; but it proclaims the sanction for them. It speaks, throughout, of men being brought under the operation of the laws of the kingdom of heaven—laws more severe than any of which they had hitherto been conscious, and of all their actions being done under the eye of a Father in heaven, who will reward or punish them in accordance with their most secret conduct. More particularly, it concludes by a clear declaration that an appointed day will come when this judgment will be executed, and that our Lord Himself will preside over its execution. 'Many will say to me in that day, Lord, Lord, have we not prophesied in Thy name? and in Thy name have cast out devils? and in Thy name done many wonderful works? And then will I profess unto them, I never knew you: depart from me, ye that work iniquity.' 'Therefore,' He adds, 'whosoever heareth these sayings of Mine, and doeth them, I will liken him unto a wise man;' and 'Every one that heareth these sayings of Mine, and doeth them not, shall be likened unto a foolish man.'

In view of this conspicuous illustration of our Lord's preaching, taken from one of His most familiar and, as some have thought, least dogmatic utterances—one, moreover, which is placed by the Evangelist in the forefront of his account of the Gospel— it can hardly be necessary to dwell on the numerous other passages in which our Lord announces more specifically and solemnly His future return in glory to execute judgment. It may serve to confirm their force, however, to observe how frequently, as in the instance just mentioned, they occur, so to say, incidentally, to support some other truth or declaration; as though the great and awful fact were ever present to our Lord's mind, and He desired it to be similarly present to the mind of His disciples, as giving to all He says the supreme sanction of His power and His will to put it into execution. It is not only that there will be a judgment, but that He will Himself execute it. What we are told by the Evangelist, again and again, is that the Son of Man will come in His glory, and will sit on the throne of His glory, and will gather together all His elect from the four winds, and all nations shall be gathered before Him, and He shall separate them as a shepherd divideth his sheep from the goats, and that He will reward every man according to his works. It was upon this declaration of His future return in power and judgment, that He was finally condemned by the Jewish Council. In reply to the adjuration of the High-priest, 'Art thou the Christ the Son of the Blessed?' Jesus said, 'I am; and hereafter ye shall see the Son of Man sitting on the right hand of power, and coming in the clouds of heaven.' 'Then the high-priest rent his clothes, and saith, What need we any further witnesses? Ye have heard the blasphemy; what think ye? And they all condemned Him to be guilty of death.'*

Now, the first observation which may be made upon a review of these awful declarations is, that they are a conclusive proof of the manner in which our Lord's claims as a moral teacher are indissolubly associated with His superhuman and divine nature. In these repeated and solemn assertions we are able to rest on broad grounds, independent of critical or philosophical disputes. Our Lord's assertions of His power and right to judge mankind, and of His future coming for that purpose, are common to all the Evangelists, and are at least as strong in St. Matthew as in St. John. The latter Evangelist, indeed, records some sayings which throw a light upon the relation in which our Lord stands to God

* St. Mark xiv. 61-64.

the Father, in His office as Judge. 'The Father,' we are told, 'judgeth no man, but hath committed all judgment unto the Son; that all men should honour the Son, even as they honour the Father. For as the Father hath life in Himself, so hath He given to the Son to have life in Himself; and hath given Him authority to execute judgment also, because He is the Son of Man.' The power of judging all men must lie in the hands of God alone, and any person who exercises that power must be endued with the omnipotence and omniscience of God Himself. St. John thus reveals the necessary condition in our Lord's relation to the Father for His exercising the office of Judge. But the declaration that He will exercise that office, and will exercise it with the whole authority and power of the Godhead, is made or implied throughout His teaching, and cannot be eliminated from any of the Gospels without such an entire annihilation of their historical character as would prevent our placing any reliance on their account of our Lord's words.

To take but one instance, consider what a tremendous claim is involved in the familiar parable of the division between the sheep and the goats. There are some persons who would use that parable, like many other portions of the Gospels, as though it were simply a touching and forcible exhortation to beneficence. But it must be apparent upon reflection how much more is involved in it. The blessing and the curse in that last awful scene are bestowed, not simply upon works of benevolence or unkindness as such, but upon works of benevolence or unkindness considered as in effect done to our Lord Himself. The parable depicts all mankind as standing in a vital relation to Christ, and as blessed or cursed according as they have served either Him or those whom He adopts as His own. Recall the final sentence of the scene, 'Then shall He answer them, saying, Verily I say unto you, Inasmuch as ye did it not to one of the least of these, ye did it not to Me. And these shall go away into everlasting punishment.' Had the speaker been only one of the sons of men, what a tremendous presumption would have been involved in such a juxtaposition of words! 'Ye did it not to Me: and these shall go away into everlasting punishment.' The whole fate of mankind depending on their relation to Him! To be the Judge of every human soul, the supreme arbiter of every act, and thought, and word—this is the character in which our Lord presents Himself to us throughout the Gospels, in some of His simplest utterances as well as in His most mysterious; and in this claim alone He reveals Himself to us as our Lord and our God.

Our Lord's office as Judge is, in fact, one of the

first great practical realities which are at stake in that long battle which has raged around the Church, and sometimes within it, from the earliest times to the present hour, respecting the nature of our Lord. We may sometimes hear that question discussed as if it were to a large extent a speculative one. That is the manner in which it was represented by Arian writers in the time of St. Athanasius; and the first ages of the Church, and the very lifetime of the Apostles, were at least as rife as the present day with attempts to create some other image of our Lord than that which is furnished by the records of His miraculous birth in St. Matthew and St. Luke, of His eternal Godhead in St. John, and of His Ascension to sit on the right hand of the Father in the Acts of the Apostles. If He were only a teacher, such attempts might not vitally conflict with His authority. But He claims to be much more than a teacher. In the very first place He claims to be a judge; and thus a debate respecting His nature involves a debate respecting His jurisdiction. He asserts a prerogative and power to which it would be blasphemy, as the High-priest declared, for a mere man to aspire, and He has indissolubly united this claim with His whole moral and spiritual teaching. That is the character in which, at the very outset as at the end of His ministry, He came before the Jews; that is the character in which His angels revealed Him as

He departed from earth; that is the character in which He comes before us now. It must, moreover, be observed that the acknowledgment or rejection of Him in that character is declared by Him to be a point on which His judgment at the last day will be pronounced with special solemnity. It was in connection with His claim to be the Christ of God, divine amidst all His humiliation, that He uttered the solemn warning, 'Whosoever shall be ashamed of Me and of My words, of him shall the Son of Man be ashamed, when He shall come in His own glory, and in His Father's, and of the holy angels.'

Accordingly we find that this principle occupies as prominent a place in the preaching of the Apostles as in that of our Lord Himself. In the crucial example of St. Paul's preaching to the Gentiles—his speech at Athens—we observe that he employs this truth as the very lever with which he would move the world. 'The times of this ignorance God winked at; but now commandeth all men everywhere to repent; because He hath appointed a day, in the which He will judge the world in righteousness by that Man whom He hath ordained; whereof He hath given assurance unto all men, in that He hath raised Him from the dead.' In writing to the Romans, the Apostle's argument at the outset speaks of the day in which God will judge the secrets of men by Jesus Christ, according to his Gospel. The day of the Lord Jesus is ever prominent in his thoughts. He reiterates that we must all stand before the judgment-seat of Christ; and he looked forward to that day for the crown of righteousness of which, at the close of his life, he could indulge a confident hope. But the Apocalypse shows us most conclusively how vast a space this truth occupied in Apostolic thought and teaching. The New Testament may almost be regarded as summed up in this vision of our Lord's return to judgment, and in His revelation as Alpha and Omega, the first and the last.

In fact, the prominence which this belief occupies in Apostolic thought is so evident, that it has even been made a ground of objection to the Apostles' authority, that they lived in an expectation, which proved to be unfounded, of our Lord's immediate return. It is probable, indeed, if we take the most natural interpretation of some of their expressions, that they were mistaken on this point. But it is the very point on which our Lord expressly said that they would be left in ignorance, and therefore liable to be mistaken; and it would seem that the particular time at which He would return to judgment in no way affects, as respects individuals, the supreme import of the fact itself. If it be a fact, it is equally important to us all, whether it be near or far off; and even if the Apostles had not been in the error supposed in point of time and date, the intensity with which their thoughts were preoccupied with the subject would have been none the less justifiable and inevitable; and we ought ourselves to enter into their feelings and share them to the full. The truth that the consummation of all things will involve a moral judgment upon every human being, and that this judgment will be pronounced by our Lord, and in accordance with His revealed will and word, is one which, wherever it is accepted, must needs overpower all other considerations. It establishes once for all a fixed and central point for human life and for each individual soul.

We may reflect with advantage upon the bearing of the principle in this respect upon the circumstances in which it was first proclaimed. The world to which the Apostles were commissioned to preach was distracted by the most various views of the object of life, the good of life, and the rule of life. As Horace describes himself, men fluctuated backwards and forwards between one philosophy and another, as thought, or fancy, or pleasure led them. The end of life was as obscure as its origin; and amidst all this doubt and vague speculation, moral energy and resolution were continually growing feebler. In this state of thought and feeling, the Apostles were able to proclaim an absolute certainty to every soul; and a certainty of the most clear and vivid character. They proclaimed, not merely in general terms, a judgment to come—a belief which all the most thoughtful heathen had anticipated—but a judgment by a particular Person, whose character and will they were able to describe, and whose claim to submission was accompanied by the most gracious assurances. All else would pass away; it would pass away to the individual, and it would come to an end in itself. But our Lord had declared that those who believed in Him, and strove to obey Him, were building their houses on an eternal rock; and that He would return to give them everlasting life, and honour, and blessing. What wonder that, in proportion as this assurance was accepted, and believed as a certainty, it absorbed the souls of men, and overbore all other influences? It gave to Christian life at once its peculiar moral character, and its special vigour and confidence. The principle of duty, of following right because of right, can never, indeed, in any decay of society, lose its hold over the more noble souls. But as the world is constituted, such a principle cannot, standing by itself, exert the same inspiring influence as when invigorated by the personal assurances of our Lord, and sustained by the conviction that He will certainly vindicate it and reward obedience to it. Alike in the old world and in the present day, in the absence of Christian faith, too many men can only do their duty in sadness of heart, and with little to comfort them under the disappointments which life must often bring them; and they are necessarily destitute of the expansion, the sympathy, and the energy of soul by which alone their own nature can be fully developed, and by which they exert their best influence upon others. But when it was proclaimed to men that the Lord Jesus Christ, in all His combined mercy and justice, would hereafter bring every work into judgment, and that His gracious and holy will was the beginning and end, the Alpha and Omega of human life, all hesitation, and irresolution, and melancholy, were at once swept away. Men could know in Whom they believed. They could study His character; they could obtain the guidance of His Spirit by prayer; they could be sure of His assistance in growing more and more like Him; and life became, for all practical purposes, clear, and hopeful, and full of peace. What does it matter to such a belief whether, as the early Christians supposed, our Lord was soon to return, or whether centuries were to elapse before His reappearance? The one important fact was that He would return, to execute judgment, to save and bless His own; and this great reality was supreme. It solved at once the main problems of existence, it settled life on an eternal basis, opened up its true sources, and enabled every one to devote himself to the lawful work of his calling in a spirit of perfect truth, freedom, and fearlessness.

For, let it be observed, the fact that this judgment of our Lord gives supreme importance to the moral and spiritual character of our actions is so far from placing it out of harmony with the business of life, that this is the only condition on which it could control all the work of life without exception. The one quality which is supreme in all work, of whatever kind, is the moral quality. Other qualities must needs vary indefinitely. The physical and intellectual powers present an endless diversity both in degree and in kind. But truth in work, and faithfulness to the domestic or social relations in which we are placed—these conditions are the same in every occupation, and in proportion as they are fulfilled, is the utmost amount of intellectual or physical power developed, and does work of all kinds prosper. The moral duties, for our discharge of which we shall be judged, are the hinges on which the whole world turns. Let those be duly performed, and everything else will follow, in accordance with the various laws which God has impressed upon our nature. We have but to seek first the kingdom of God and His righteousness, and all secondary things shall be added unto us. The whole of life, therefore, without any exception, was illuminated and revivified by this revelation of our Lord as the Judge of quick and dead.

In proportion as we grasp the same principle, and make it the starting-point of all our thought, shall we be sensible of a similar illumination and a similar vigour. We need to maintain that grasp in two respects—alike with reference to those general discussions respecting the conduct and the organization of life, which are forced upon our attention by the literature and thought of the time, and in respect to our private lives. In regard to the former, it cannot but be the duty of a Christian to adopt a more decided tone than that to which, from feelings of mistaken kindness, and, perhaps, of misplaced modesty, we are often inclined. From the point of view of the great truth we have been considering, nothing, surely, can be more lamentable, than that such a vast amount of time and energy should be consumed in the constant discussion of moral and religious problems on other than Christian principles. On those principles, no philosophy can reach a true result, no moral system can lead to sound conclusions, no system of education, whether private or national, whether at home, or in schools, or in Universities, can be trusted, which is not based upon the recognition of our Lord as the centre of all God's purposes, and as the Judge of all mankind.

He claims to have declared the moral principles by which all mankind will be judged, by which every act and word and thought will be measured, and consequently to have determined the eternal standard and rule of moral action.

It is indeed the glory of the Gospel, or rather it is our Lord's glory, that every truth, of whatever kind, belongs to Him—is a part of His wisdom and His will; and just as the greatest Christian Fathers regarded the philosophy of Greece as sharing in some degree with the Law of Moses the office of being a schoolmaster to the world to bring it unto Christ, so whatever moral truths may be established by independent speculation must needs be so many additional steps on the road towards Him who is the Truth. But this does not alter the fact that it is alike our privilege and our duty, in the present day, to start on every subject from the central truth that our Saviour is the Lord and Judge of all men, to estimate every moral and religious argument or opinion by the standard of His words, and to depend wholly on the promised aid of His Spirit to guide us aright. We cannot allow less than this to a principle of so absolute and supreme a character as that which we have been contemplating. It may be pressed too far, or injudiciously applied, as it was in the Middle Ages, when physical questions were determined by doubtful inferences from theological premises. But we have of late been certainly tending towards the other extreme, and such reflections as these may well suggest to us a reconsideration of our position and our duty in the matter. There is one moral and religious question which must take precedence of all others, and that is the old one, 'What think ye of Christ?' Do you accept His claim to be the Judge of quick and dead, and the Lord of life alike in this world and in the next? He comes forward with that claim, and there is no similar claim in competition with it. If a man unhappily reject it, he can only fall back on the comparatively dim light of nature and of conscience, and feel his way in the twilight as best he may. But it is a claim which may be said to be in possession of the ground. During the last eighteen centuries it has guided the civilization which is now the hope of the world, and there is an enormous presumption in its favour. But if it be accepted, it decides at one trenchant stroke many of the controversies by which the world is distracted; it sets aside many a futile debate; and it affords a firm basis for the edifice of moral and social life.

But, to turn for a moment from this more general view of the principle in question to its relation to our private lives, we must acknowledge at once how profound and how elevating would be its influence if it were always present to our minds in full force.

To believe that everything we do, or say, or think, is under the eye of the Lord Jesus Christ, and will hereafter be revealed at His tribunal, and judged by Him—this would seem, without controversy, the mightiest moral influence that can be brought to bear upon a man. It was said of late, by a distinguished writer who was not a Christian, that our Lord's character was so perfect that a man could hardly adopt a better rule for his guidance than that of acting in such a manner that Christ, if He saw his actions, would approve them. But what is this to the positive belief that Christ does see them, and will approve or condemn them in proportion as they are in accordance with His will? There was always something vague and uncertain, both among Jews and heathen, in the belief of a future judgment. It was, perhaps, something too vast, too intangible, too much beyond our standard and measure, to be realized, and to produce its due influence upon the mind. But to be judged by the Man Christ Jesus, whose words we read in the Gospels, whose voice penetrates into our hearts, Who is portrayed so vividly that we can almost see and hear Him—to believe that this same Jesus will so return in like manner as He was seen to go into heaven—to be brought into His presence, to feel His eye and His judgment upon us, and to await His censure or His approval—this is a prospect which we can realize only too keenly, and which is fitted to touch the very depths of our souls. Indeed, the thought of that penetrating judgment would be unsupportable unless it were accompanied by the assurance that this Judge is also our Saviour, alike now and hereafter. We may be assured that He will display towards us the mercy as well as the severity which marked His words and acts when He was upon earth, and we cannot doubt the love and tenderness of One who laid down His life for us.

The blessing, accordingly, of this revelation is as great for the present as for the future. Were we left alone, even with the guidance which the Gospels and the Epistles afford us, to work out our own salvation, to train and discipline ourselves in harmony with the Saviour's holy will, we should be appalled at the consciousness of our weakness and our ignorance. But the Lord, who requires us to grow like Him, and who has established His will as the final standard of our lives, is ever present with us, to guide us by His Spirit into all truth, alike of thought and of action. If we trust Him, and strive continually to obey Him, His final judgment will prove but the last act of the gracious discipline by which He has all our lives been bringing us into ever-increasing harmony with Himself. He does not ask us, with all our sins and imperfections, to bring ourselves into harmony with Him. He asks us only to submit ourselves to Him in trust, in prayer, and in faithful study of His word, and He Himself will bring us into that harmony. Our whole thoughts in meditating on this subject may be thus summed up in the prayer of the *Te Deum*: 'Thou sittest at the right hand of God, in the glory of the Father. We believe that Thou shalt come to be our Judge. We therefore pray Thee, help Thy servants, whom Thou hast redeemed with Thy precious blood.'

LECTURE IX

THE GIFT OF THE SPIRIT

"Verily, verily, I say unto you, he that believeth on Me, the works that I do shall he do also; and greater works than these shall he do, because I go unto My Father."—*John* xiv. 12.

THE Ascension of our Lord must be regarded, for its due appreciation, in reference to the manifestations which had preceded it on the one hand, and to those which followed it on the other. It is not an event which stands by itself, but it is part of a continuous manifestation of the Saviour's life and power. It is, in the first place, only the final and more solemn assumption of a condition of glory into which He had entered at His rising from the grave. The significance of our Lord's Resurrection is nowhere presented in the New Testament as consisting in the mere fact of His having risen from the sepulchre, like those whom He had Himself raised from the dead. It is not to that bare fact that the Apostles bear testimony, but to the fact of His having risen in glory and power. As has been observed in a previous Lecture, they do not even proclaim the Resurrection until they are able to point to the miraculous powers over men's bodies and souls which had been exerted through them, as proofs that their Lord was exalted to be a Prince and a Saviour. It is in harmony with this, that all accounts of our Saviour's appearances to the disciples, after the Resurrection, represent Him, not merely as having been raised from corruption, but as endued with powers and qualities superior to those He exercised before, and essentially different from those which other men have enjoyed. Everywhere He appears, not merely as the risen, but as the glorified, Lord. His body, indeed, no less than His soul, retains what we may venture to call its identity. It retains the mark of the wound in the side and the print of the nails; it is recognized instinctively, by voice as well as by sight, except when He purposely throws a veil around Himself. The eyes of those whom He visits may be holden for a time, that they should not know Him, but some sudden touch reveals Him, and then they recall many indications that it is the same Lord with whom they had lived. But He is nevertheless freed from some of the most conspicuous limitations which are attached to our own bodies, and to which He had Himself submitted during His previous life. He appears suddenly in the midst of His disciples, although the doors are shut; He vanishes as suddenly out of the sight of the two disciples at

Emmaus; He would seem to manifest His presence whenever and wherever He would, and appears superior to all ordinary bodily necessities. His Ascension into the heavens, exhibiting a supremacy over the ordinary laws of matter, is but the last and most conspicuous of these numerous evidences of His having entered by His Resurrection, in body as well as in spirit, into a new and glorified condition. Whatever manifestations, in short, are recorded of Him, exhibit Him as having assumed an entirely new state of bodily and spiritual existence—an existence one indeed with His former state of humiliation, but completely freed from its restrictions. He appears to transcend the limitations of the flesh, no less than to have burst the bonds of the grave; and from the time of His Resurrection, while remaining man, He possessed a life, and exerted a power, infinitely above those of our present humanity.*

It would seem, in fact, that we have an exact and vivid description of the change which had thus passed over the body of our Lord in St. Paul's grand description of the resurrection body of Christians. The appearances of our Lord after His Resurrection, and the fact of the Ascension itself, are visible illustrations of the Apostle's argument, that 'all flesh is not the same flesh,' but that, as there is one kind

---

* See Dr. Milligan on *The Resurrection of our Lord*, Lect. I. pp. 10–24.

of flesh of men and another flesh of beasts, another of fishes, and another of birds; as there are also celestial bodies and bodies terrestrial, but the glory of the celestial is one, and the glory of the terrestrial is another; so also, is the resurrection of the dead. 'It is sown in corruption, it is raised in incorruption; it is sown in dishonour, it is raised in glory; it is sown in weakness, it is raised in power; it is sown a natural body, it is raised a spiritual body. There is a natural body and there is a spiritual body. And so it is written, the first man Adam was made a living soul; the last Adam was made a quickening spirit.' In those words the Apostle presents our Lord, in His glorified state, as being as distinctly a type of the spiritual body, animated by the quickening spirit, as Adam was of the earthly body, animated by the living soul. A spiritual influence, infinitely superior to that which is exhibited in our present earthly frame, will hereafter animate those who rise in Christ, and will transform them; 'and as we have borne the image of the earthy, we shall also bear the image of the heavenly.' That image was actually seen in our Lord, in the complete transformation which His body underwent, though remaining one with that body which suffered and was buried. He rose and ascended, as our Article states, quoting His own words, 'with flesh, bones, and all things appertaining to the perfection of man's nature'—'Handle Me and see,' He said, 'for a spirit hath not flesh and bones, as ye see Me have'—but all these elements of man's nature perfected, glorified, placed in new relations, and endued with a new life. There is thus no essentially greater wonder in the Ascension than in our Lord's various appearances before it. It was His last solemn farewell to His disciples; it marked the moment when He assumed the full exercise of that power which He had won by death, and it was thus distinguished by circumstances equally striking in themselves and symbolical of His exaltation. But it is an event substantially one in character with those which had preceded it since the Resurrection; it is indissolubly united with them, and rests on the same evidence.

But this manifestation of the Saviour's glory in respect to His bodily nature is accompanied by a similar assumption of power in the moral and spiritual sphere. He himself, indeed, needed no glorification in this respect. His previous humiliation had affected His bodily state only, and His spiritual and moral glory was as great before His Resurrection as after it. Even while the Word was made flesh, and dwelt among us in the ordinary conditions of human flesh and blood, those who had pure hearts beheld His glory, the glory as of the only begotten of the Father, full of grace and truth.

But that moral and spiritual power which He did not need for Himself He did need for others. It is clearly revealed in the Gospels, alike by the evidence of experience and by express statements, that His power to influence the hearts of men, and to quicken them into true moral life by spiritual influences, was exercised under limitations and restrictions during the period of His ministry and before His death and resurrection. St. John expressly tells us, in reference to one of His great promises, 'This spake He of the Spirit, which they that believe on Him should receive; for the Holy Ghost was not yet given, because that Jesus was not yet glorified.' The same truth is repeatedly urged by our Lord Himself in His last discourses to His disciples. 'It is expedient for you,' He says, 'that I go away: for if I go not away the Comforter will not come unto you; but if I depart, I will send Him unto you.' This truth, it may be observed, affords perhaps the most striking of all illustrations of the immense efficacy and supreme necessity of the atoning work of our Lord in His death on the Cross. It was indispensable for the manifestation of God's justice that the natural consequences of man's sin should be allowed to work themselves out, as they did by the rejection and crucifixion of our Lord, and that He should take upon Himself those consequences, before God could interpose, as He had from the first purposed, to deliver mankind by the supernatural operation of His Spirit from the ruin which they had brought upon themselves by their revolt from Him. It was necessary that Christ should be 'set forth to be a propitiation through faith in His blood, to declare the righteousness of God for the remission of sins that are past, through the forbearance of God; to declare,' the Apostle insists, 'at this time His righteousness; that He might be just, and the justifier of him that believeth in Jesus.' When this had been done, and when our Lord could pass in His glorified humanity into the presence of the Father, there pleading His sufferings, of which His body still bore the marks, as a sufficient penalty and atonement for human evil, then was it possible for God, through Him, to set free that gracious influence of His Spirit from which the sins of men had hitherto debarred them. Christ, by His perfect obedience and Atonement, had won that gift; and the Spirit was henceforth, if we may so speak, placed in His hands as the reward of His work, to be by Him bestowed upon all who submitted themselves to Him in faith. In this respect the Saviour was glorified at the Ascension in His moral and spiritual no less than in His bodily nature. He possesses a power which he could not exert before; He is able to give the Comforter to His disciples, and that Spirit henceforth proceeds from the Father and the Son, to exercise over the spirits and souls, and ultimately over the bodies, of Christians His transforming and transfiguring influences.

These considerations, it will be found, bring light and unity into the various sayings of our Lord which are recorded between His Resurrection and Ascension. The burden of His repeated sayings to His disciples is that He bestows on them henceforth new and irresistible spiritual powers. One of His first utterances, when He came and stood in the midst of them while they were assembled in secret for fear of the Jews, was, 'Peace be unto you. As My Father hath sent Me, even so send I you. And when He had said this He breathed on them, and said unto them, Receive ye the Holy Ghost.' He could bestow that gift then as He could not bestow it before. He bids them teach all nations, baptizing them in the Name of the Father and of the Son and of the Holy Ghost, bringing them therefore under the life-giving influences of those three sacred Persons, setting free, if the expression may be permitted, the whole power of the Godhead to work upon them. St. Luke accordingly, in the Acts, represents His instructions to the Apostles during the interval between His Resurrection and Ascension as mainly having reference to this promise. 'Being assembled together with them, He commanded them that they should not depart from Jerusalem, but wait for the promise of the Father, which, saith He, ye have heard of Me.' Every message, every act, leads up to this great promise, as that in which the whole work of the Saviour was to be fulfilled. The Apostles, in a word, are not commissioned to go forth into the world as teachers only, but as men endued with new powers themselves and bringing new powers to others. That which they had seen of the glorification of our Lord's body was to be an example and a pledge to them of the work which was to be wrought in men's souls. A new creative influence was to be set at work by means of it, and the moral and spiritual life of all who submitted to the Saviour was to be regenerated. When, accordingly, we are told that 'with great power gave the Apostles witness of the resurrection of the Lord Jesus,' it is added, 'and great grace was upon them all.' The power did not lie in the mere force of their testimony to the fact of our Lord having risen from the grave, but in their testimony to Him as a glorified and ascended Lord, and in the great grace which He bestowed on all who submitted to Him.

This is an aspect of the revelation of the New Testament which is peculiarly liable to be obscured amidst the controversies of the present time, and which it is essential for us above all things to keep in view if we would meet the difficulties which those controversies present to us. The main effort of all schools of thought which have struggled against the full supernatural revelation of the Gospel has been to concentrate attention on the moral teaching of the New Testament, and to separate it from the miraculous narratives with which it is accompanied. But all such attempts fail to grapple with that which, if the facts be fully realized, may well appear the greatest miracle of all. That fact is the event to which this season bears witness—the sudden creation of a new spiritual life, of new moral energies and powers, after the descent of the Holy Spirit on the day of Pentecost. By no conceivable process of criticism can the fact of such a sudden creation be explained away. So far as the life of believers is concerned, it is impossible not to feel that we enter into a new world as we pass from the Gospels to the Acts of the Apostles and the Epistles. In the history of the Gospels even the disciples of our Lord are marked to the last by a weakness, a narrowness, and even a worldliness, which is in amazing contrast with the infinite spiritual grace of our Lord Himself. At the last moment before His Ascension they recur to these mere worldly expectations, saying, 'Lord, wilt Thou at this time restore again the kingdom to Israel?' Equally striking is the absence in the Gospels of any evidence that our Lord's perfect moral and spiritual teaching produced the effect of regenerating, to any appreciable extent, the lives of more than a few, and a very few, devoted followers. He gathers no church about Him, and the moment He dies His whole work seems for the moment to be at an end. Nor is the case different after His Resurrection, even the spiritual insight of the Apostles, as has just been mentioned, being still imperfect. But after the Ascension, and the gift of the Holy Spirit which followed it, the Apostles are enabled instantly to gather around them some thousands of followers, whose Christian graces have been the ideal of the whole Church ever since. Picture to yourselves, on the one hand, that hardened society of Scribes and Pharisees, and that fickle and passionate mob, by whom our Lord, notwithstanding all the grace and power of His teaching, was condemned to death; and, on the other, that body of about three thousand souls who were added to the Church the very day of the descent of the Holy Spirit, and who 'continued steadfastly in the Apostles' doctrine and fellowship,' who 'were of one heart and of one soul,' and who were animated by the same gracious influences of love, joy, and peace.

Do not these wonderful manifestations of spiritual grace exactly correspond to our Lord's promise in the text—'He that believeth on Me, the works that I do shall he do also; and greater works than these shall he do, because I go unto My Father'? Were they not an exact fulfilment of the assurance, 'It is expedient for you that I go away: for if I go not away the Comforter will not come unto you; but if I depart I will send Him unto you. And when He is come, He will reprove the world of sin, and of righteousness, and of judgment.' Then it was that those who listened to St. Peter 'were pricked in their heart, and said unto Peter and to the rest of the Apostles, "Men and brethren, what shall we do?"' and Peter was able to reply, 'Repent, and be baptized every one of you in the name of Jesus Christ for the remission of sins, and ye shall receive the gift of the Holy Ghost.' Unquestionably the moral and spiritual power exerted by the Apostles after the descent of the Holy Spirit produced greater works—far more conspicuous and more enduring results—than all the teaching of our Lord during His lifetime, notwithstanding the miraculous manifestations by which it was attested. This is, after all, the decisive fact of Christian experience, and perhaps the chief practical evidence of our Faith. The undoubted facts of Christian history bear irresistible testimony to the truth that, after our Lord's death and resurrection, a new spiritual life was at work in the world, transfiguring the lives of those who faithfully submitted to it, just as our Lord's body was transformed and glorified. Henceforth, it was evident, Christians were not living merely by their own powers as they had lived before, subject only to the intellectual and moral influences of Christian teaching. But they were in the hands of a life-giving Spirit, from whom they drew continual supplies of new spiritual energy.

With the evidence of the Epistles in our hands, bearing witness to the intense spiritual and moral beauty of Christian life as represented in the teaching and the practice of the Apostles, it is strange men should fail to acknowledge the presence of this new and life-giving influence. We seem to behold the Divine Spirit breathing over the moral chaos —to hear the Divine command, 'Let there be light!' and to see that it was fulfilled—'and there was light.' It is, indeed, but too natural and easy to point to facts which appear to conflict with this gracious truth, and which render it sometimes difficult of belief. Where are the signs, men may ask, of the continued existence and operation of this transforming influence in the subsequent history of the Church and in our own day? If such a spiritual power as that we have been considering —a power like that which transfigured our Lord's bodily nature, and which transformed the lives of the Apostles and early Christians—has been at work in the Church ever since, and is at work within it now, how are we to account for the frequent and grievous decay of Christian virtue, for the scandals which in age after age have disgraced Christendom? How is it that such powers are not so conspicuous among us at this moment as to silence all objection, and to compel men to confess that the Spirit of God is with us of a truth?

As I will observe in a moment, it is too easy to account for this sad contrast, for this failure to realize the Christian ideal. But we may boldly say, in the first place, that, grievous as are these defects in our practice, grievous as they ever have been in the history of the Church, history nevertheless does, on the whole, bear the most conspicuous witness to the ever-present influence of this Spirit of Grace. It can certainly be said, without fear of contradiction, that in every age since the first preaching of the Gospel to the present time, a succession of saints has been maintained, not unworthy to be enrolled with those of the primitive Church. They have been fewer or more obscure at one time than another, but no one acquainted with the course of ecclesiastical history will deny their continuous existence. The life of this brotherhood of saints has flowed on in a perennial stream, pure and gracious in itself, and bringing vitality to the arid wastes of natural society, or corrupt Christianity, which lay around its course. Connected with this, and as a consequence of it, is another fact equally

conspicuous throughout the Christian ages—that of
a power of constant revival and reformation within
the Christian Church. This, it must be owned, on
candid consideration, is a unique phenomenon in
human experience. In all history, except that in
which the Church has been the prominent influence, the law of development has been that which
prevails in the natural world, of growth up to
a certain point, followed by decay. One nation
after another has come on the stage of the world's
history, and each has brought some new contribution
to its life, some new energy, moral or intellectual.
Egypt, Greece, and Rome, for instance, have thus
succeeded one another, and each has established for
a time an imposing civilization. But in each case
the civilization became corrupt, and when that
corruption had once set in, there was no power of
resistance or renovation. But the history of Christendom—a history which is now that of eighteen
centuries—is that of a succession of reformations of
moral and intellectual life. There is no race,
neither Greek, nor Roman, nor Celtic, nor German,
which has not from time to time felt this reforming
and regenerating power, and which has not thus
been enabled to cast off its corruptions and enter
on a new career. It was by the influence of the
Church, as no impartial historian will question, that
out of the corrupted elements of the Greek and

Roman world, and the fierce and untamed energies of the Teutonic races, the grand and enduring fabric of our present civilization was built up. The moral and spiritual energies of Christian missionaries exerted a creative force and a power of control which were lacking alike to Greek arts and to Roman arms, and they thus sowed the seeds of an ever-growing Christendom. All other civilizations and faiths have fallen into decay, while this alone exhibits the elements of an enduring vitality.

In proportion, indeed, as the simple truths of the Gospel have been obscured by human ignorance, or misused by human ambition for unworthy ends, have these gracious influences of God's Spirit been lost. But the Church has never long been without her prophets, to revive the truth and to set free anew the springs of Christian life. The work of the great saints of the early Church and of the Middle Ages was revived by the great leaders of the Reformation; and the Evangelical succession, reinvigorated through the spiritual insight of the Reformers, has never since been interrupted. The Church, in short, has succeeded in taking up into itself members of all nations in all ages, and in moulding them into members of her own body, constituent parts of the same great Christian creation. It is this feeling—often unconscious, but this alone—which gives to modern life its hopefulness and energy. The history of the Church in the past forbids us to despair of the moral and spiritual renovation of any people whatever; and thus we work and struggle, alike at home and abroad, in the hope of a continuous progress.

But, while this is true, and is a sufficient answer to the objections I have mentioned, we must none the less admit a grievous falling short in our realization of those spiritual powers we have been considering; and the reason must be familiar to us all. Our Lord proceeds after the text to say, 'And whatsoever ye shall ask in My name, that will I do, that the Father may be glorified in the Son. If ye shall ask anything in My name, I will do it.' It need not be said that this asking in Christ's name implies no ordinary or cursory petition; it involves earnest, devout, and constant prayer, in that spirit of faith, and that striving and wrestling for spiritual graces, which our Lord Himself displayed in the days of His flesh, and which His Apostles urge on us as indispensable for obtaining an answer to prayer. 'Let a man ask in faith,' says St. James, 'nothing wavering. For he that wavereth is like a wave of the sea, driven with the wind and tossed. For let not that man think that he shall receive anything of the Lord;' and he tells us that it is the effectual fervent prayer of a righteous man which availeth much. If, then, any of us ask, or if we are asked, Where is the moral and spiritual grace which should transform our lives, as they transformed those of the first Christians? let the questioner ask himself whether he is conscious of that supreme devotion to the kingdom of God, and that craving, above all things, for righteousness, which impels him to the incessant and earnest prayer in answer to which alone this grace is promised. One essential character of the operation of the Spirit of God is that His grace never works mechanically. He speaks indeed to the heart. He touches the springs of the conscience, and is thus ever arousing in each of us a craving for grace and truth; but His further influences are dependent on the degree in which we yield to those gentle invitations. But the history of the Acts of the Apostles, confirmed as it is in all ages by Christian experience, may give us a firm assurance that this spiritual power, or rather that Holy Spirit and that gracious Lord, are here, and ever at our side; that we owe it to Their grace alone that we are not worse than we are, and that, in proportion as we yield to Them, in proportion as we are able by Their aid to set our affections on things above, and to appeal to Them in faith and prayer, They will give us larger measure of this grace, and will help us to transform our lives. The Holy Spirit is still given, as in the days of the early Church, to those who truly seek Him. May God give us grace thus to strive after the likeness of Christ, and thus to realize it, that 'like as we do believe our Lord Jesus Christ to have ascended into the heavens, so we may also in heart and mind thither ascend, and with Him continually dwell.'

THE END.

www.ingramcontent.com/pod-product-compliance
Lightning Source LLC
Chambersburg PA
CBHW051921160426
43198CB00012B/1993